Bill Barnes
6/23/05

HEALING AMERICA

*Values and Vision
for the 21st Century*

PAUL SIMON

ORBIS BOOKS
Maryknoll, New York 10545

Founded in 1970, Orbis Books endeavors to publish works that enlighten the mind, nourish the spirit, and challenge the conscience. The publishing arm of the Maryknoll Fathers and Brothers, Orbis seeks to explore the global dimensions of the Christian faith and mission, to invite dialogue with diverse cultures and religious traditions, and to serve the cause of reconciliation and peace. The books published reflect the views of their authors and do not represent the official position of the Maryknoll Society. To learn more about Maryknoll and Orbis Books, please visit our website at www.maryknoll.org.

Library of Congress Cataloging-in-Publication Data

Simon, Paul, 1928-
  Healing America : values and vision for the 21st century / Paul
Simon.
     p. cm.
Includes bibliographical references and index.
  ISBN 1-57075-505-1
  1. Values—United States. 2. Conduct of life—United States. I.
Title.
  BJ353.V35 S56 2003
  303.3'72'0973—dc21
                                             2003009843

To Bill Austin
Hearing-aid pioneer and humanitarian

CONTENTS

CONTENTS

Acknowledgments

The idea for this book came from Michael Leach, my editor and publisher on several books. His suggestions enriched the manuscript. Among others who helped were Gene Callahan, David Christensen, Kathy Fahey, Pam Gwaltney, Robert Harper, John Hayward, John Jackson, Perry Knop, Mike Lawrence, John Marty, Kenneth Millard, Arthur Simon, Patti Simon, and Sheila Simon. As in all my recent books, Marilyn Lingle deciphered my typing and hand-written notes and did it without complaint—at least to me. I am sure there are others I should be thanking. To the mentioned and unmentioned, my gratitude. They helped with the final product, but the decisions and flaws are my responsibility, not theirs.

FOREWORD

Martin E. Marty

The shelf of books devoted to terror, war, conflict, argument, and schism grows exponentially. This book does not belong on such a shelf.

Senator Paul Simon makes reference to all of the above dark themes, and his positive and constructive statements make no sense apart from the background of the tensions and upheavals of our day.

However, instead of burdening those shelves further, he rather daringly chooses the concept of healing. I say that is daring, that he is taking some risk, because to go as much against the stream as he does takes some courage. In a time when cynicism, macho declarations, and put-downs of reconcilers are what make headlines, there is a danger that anyone who sees and points to signs of hope will be dismissed as a Polyanna. The need for such writing is so urgent, however, that Simon ventures forth anyhow.

Readers who for a few hours are ready to suspend disbelief, who allow for some belief that something positive could work out, are in for surprises and treats. Unfashionably, the retired senator does not join the company of the whiners and moaners who see our culture in ruin and point clearly to the villains, always "others," who brought the ruin about.

Instead, he offers what I call "realistic hope," a more accurate term than the one he chose for a chapter title, "Optimism." He discerns movements, people, trends, and ideas that we the public can use to restore and refresh the culture.

The key to his approach appears in what looks like a throwaway line in his chapter on religion: "My own non-theologian's view of religion is that when it evokes a meanness of spirit, it is flawed; that is a distortion of faith." His self-definition is inaccurate: he is an astute theologian in the public realm. What I take from the paragraphs surrounding that line is that this is not the book in which to write a full-length study of comparative religion. There is no space here for him to enter into a "my-religion-is-better'n-your-religion" set of taunts. He has his own Christian convictions, but his generosity of spirit based on a decades-long career of negotiating in the fields of partisan politics, ideological conflict, and tension among the faiths, is evident.

One side of Paul Simon is very conservative. (He even admits to the use of a clunky old manual typewriter, and is evidently not ready to enter the computer age three decades late.) These chapters include much evidence that he would retrieve neglected goods from the past, which is what lively conservatives do. In politics, he is classified as a liberal. But after half a century of Simon-watching, I have to say that he exemplifies one style of political and ideological rhetoric that is in too rare supply. It may well be that the fundamental divide within our culture is not between liberal/conservative but between mean/non-mean.

Now, non-mean can all be in the eye of the beholder and can reflect the prejudices the beholder brings. It can look soft and compromising to the tough-minded swaggerers who write columns or run for office. But he illustrates enough that one can see that it is a kind of substantive category. Those who, in religion, culture, or politics, "evoke a meanness of spirit" do deny something of potential healing power in the character of religious, cultural, or political endeavors.

I've made a site-visit to the institute that Professor Simon's work has inspired at Southern Illinois University and seen the walls of his home, where autographed pictures of almost every president of the United States serve as reminders of struggles for justice in the American past. Whoever would follow him on the lecture or consulting trail would soon tire. He is a busy senior. Yet, as the pages that follow will make clear, he also keeps up on his reading. If some of his references have to do with timely, often ephemeral sources, it is also clear that he has read widely and deeply, above all in Alexis de Tocqueville and Abraham Lincoln. He puts to work their prescriptions for healing in times of conflict.

Simon has a proper didactic impulse. Like one of the twentieth century's great journalist-politicians-philosophers (which is what Simon also is), José Ortega y Gasset, he engages in civic pedagogy. But if his first impulse is to get us readers to think about better ways to advance our society, he also turns practical and provides clues and directions for a new agenda for action.

The senator now and then turns personal and mentions elements of his private life, including reference to his father. So let me insert a few lines on the personal side. My son John Marty, state senator in Minnesota, began his political career as an intern to Paul Simon, and has chosen him as mentor and exemplar in reform politics. I recall an early mention: John, during his intern year, wrote in our family round-robin about how he was researching and drafting legislation that would lead to enforcement of certain locomotive warning lights. The Simon staff projected that if the legislation passed and the policy went into effect, from eleven to fifteen lives would be saved every year. Of course, he added, those whose lives were saved would not know that it was the senator who helped save them, and they might not even know that there was something from which they had to be saved. But it was one tiny illustration of what it was about politics that brought satisfaction to Simon, who *would* be aware of the lives saved.

Awareness of that, wrote John, was part of what inspired him to embark on a career in politics and public service. I know of many other public servants in the two generations that follow Simon who also drew inspiration from his example. People of our age often signal to each other a wish on the lines of *ad multos annos!* May there be many more years of Simonology, which means public service in controversial areas—and nothing mean or demeaning in sight. In fact, odds are good that there would be healing.

INTRODUCTION

It is now a truism to say that "September 11th changed our world." We share an unsettled spirit, a sense of foreboding about uncertainties ahead. Today's realities, which are not all pleasant, we can tolerate, but the fear of the unknown casts a shadow over today's certainties. We sense a need to move beyond bandaging to healing our wounds.

Is there a way for us as a people to help bring more stability, peace, and harmony to our world?

There is, and we can find it not outside ourselves but in the values we have inherited. Since September 11th Americans are becoming increasingly aware of an urgency to reflect and act on the best of those values.

Not every American value has been good. Keeping people in subjection through slavery had economic value, and too often in our history people have twisted economic values into the appearance of moral values. Sometimes these values coincide, but often they do not. We tried to cover our treatment of Native Americans with a veneer of moral arguments, but history removed that veneer. We (men, that is) looked to holy scriptures to justify denying women the right to vote and defended legal segregation of the races as "God's plan," since otherwise God "wouldn't have given us different colors."

But our deepest values helped us to build a great country, and they can guide us still toward a better world. Some of these qualities are so much assumed—like self-restraint in governing ourselves

—that their value recedes from our vision. We take them for granted. We easily lose sight of the thousands of small ways in which our democracy has adapted successfully to reality. "Little things" that are part of our culture come from more than two centuries of practicing and refining democracy. They are so much more than aspects of our elections or our commercial culture. For instance, most Americans obey the spirit of the law even when there is no one around to observe their conduct. They respect the rights of others.

When I speak to a Rotary Club or a university assembly or a PTA meeting, I do so without fear of being arrested for what I say, a value so much a part of our culture it does not occur to us that for much of the world things are dramatically different.

When I write about American values, it is not in the sense that we have a monopoly on certain virtues. Many people who live under harsh dictatorships value freedom more than most Americans who take this gift as something as certain as the air they breathe. But it is now more urgent than ever for us to re-examine and renew our best values—values not often discussed on TV talk-shows, values like humility, compassion, equality of opportunity, participation, integrity, and respect. The best way to be a beacon to the world is to keep on becoming our best selves.

This book asks us to look in a mirror, but to see deeper than appearances—to recognize and repair our blemishes but also to behold the virtues that are already ours. The positive values that we have inherited can be a quiet but powerful force for good. However, there is a big "if": *if* we combine those values with a vision of the kind of a nation and world we want, and then work for that vision. I tell my political science students at Southern Illinois University that there are two vital questions that will not change their grades but may change their lives: What kind of a world do you want to live in? What are you willing to do to achieve it? Those two questions underlie the pages in this book.

Our national community of three hundred million is part of the world family of more than six billion. We lead militarily; we lead economically. Can we lead in values that will give our children and future generations a greater chance to live in a world of peace and justice and opportunity? Can we lead in sensitivity to those struggling to simply survive in much of the world? After the World Trade Center shock, like everyone, I glowed with pride when I saw signs appearing spontaneously—sometimes hand-made—with the simple message: God Bless America. But I would feel even better to see signs that read: God Bless America and the Rest of the World. We cannot "go it alone." If we can provide international leadership in the values we cherish, that will dwarf in importance our economic and military contributions, though all are entwined.

If the world's most powerful nation renews these values and has a vision of what we can do to build a better society and a better world, our country will be an immeasurably greater constructive force. My hope is that people in our country will benefit from this examination, and that at least a few in other countries might become more aware of our striving for goodness and good will. We can learn from our history; we can learn from each other. And others will see our hopes for the best in us by our good example.

CHAPTER ONE

EQUALITY

We hold these truths to be self-evident, that all men are created equal, that they are endowed by their Creator with certain inalienable rights, that among these are life, liberty and the pursuit of happiness. That to secure these rights, governments are instituted among men, deriving their just powers from the consent of the governed.

—From the Declaration of Independence, 1776

The novel idea and successful experiment to build toward a classless and free society in the New World excited citizens in the colonies that became our states, and it intrigued and inspired people in other nations. We had the good fortune to have an unusually competent, articulate, and respected group of leaders. They not only excited and lifted hopes more than two centuries ago, but, as Admiral William Crowe, former chairman of the Joint Chiefs of Staff of the United States, commented, ultimately victory in the Cold War occurred because of their ideas, not because of arms.[1] In China, students who carried a modified replica of the Statue of Liberty in Tiananmen Square did not simply carry the imitation of a statue, they carried the ideal of freedom that it represented—an idea that the Chinese leadership knew was contagious and might threaten their authoritarian rule.

1

Columnist Mark Shields, in commenting about the days preceding the fall of the Berlin Wall, noted: "These young patriots in squares like Prague and Budapest and Warsaw did not quote great European philosophers; they quoted Thomas Jefferson, they quoted Patrick Henry, they quoted Abraham Lincoln, they quoted John Kennedy, and yes, they quoted Ronald Reagan."[2]

The basic documents and the early letters of those who founded our nation make clear their love of liberty—but freedom did not extend universally to women, African Americans, Native Americans and for many years did not apply with equal legal force to immigrants from China and Japan and other Asian and African nations.

The Immigration Act of 1924 established quotas for people who wanted to come to this country, but the quotas had distinctive Western European and religious tilts. Germany had a quota of 51,227, China 100, Sweden 9,561, Morocco 100, Ireland 28,567, Egypt 100, Great Britain 34,007, South Africa 100, Norway 6,453, India 100. It is a lengthy list, written into the law, but the pattern is clear. Fortunately for our nation, immigration laws have improved since then.

We were—and are—inconsistent in the application of our ideals. It is true for any collection of human beings. It is true for each of us individually. Our Declaration of Independence starts with the ringing words, "All men are created equal . . ." At least some of those who signed that historic document believed those words to mean: All humanity is created equal. Jefferson tried unsuccessfully to ban slavery in his state of Virginia. When the Continental Congress convened in 1784, he attempted to outlaw slavery in all new states, starting in the year 1800, "except as punishment for a crime."[3] It failed by one vote, and had a delegate from New Jersey who opposed slavery been present, it would have carried. How different our history might have been! That 1784 vote indicated that the full meaning of the phrase, "All men are created equal," had substantial support, even though the Constitution adopted three years later is almost totally silent on the slavery question. In Jefferson's first presidential inaugural address, he spoke of "equal justice to all men of whatever state or persuasion."[4] The Declaration of Independence phrase expressed an important ideal. We are a better nation because we profess that value which lifts our vision and improves our conduct, even though we do not always live up to that goal.

Alexis de Tocqueville, the French visitor to the United States fifty years after our founding—who came originally to study our prisons—noted that the early colonists had come from England with its rigid feudal classes. He wrote: "While the hierarchy of rank despotically classed the inhabitants of the mother country, the colony approximated more and more the novel spectacle of a community homogenous in all its parts. A democracy, more perfect than antiquity has dared to dream of, started in full size and panoply from the midst of an ancient feudal society."[5] Over and over Tocqueville returns to the theme that equality is the great contribution the United States is making to the world, and is its great strength, but he sees slavery particularly and the treatment of free African Americans in the North as great inconsistencies that could shatter this amazingly successful experiment. He reports this conversation:

> I said one day to an inhabitant of Pennsylvania: "Be so good as to explain to me how it happens that in a state founded by Quakers and celebrated for its toleration, free blacks are not allowed to exercise civil rights. They pay taxes; is it not fair that they should vote?"
>
> "You insult us," replied the informant, "if you imagine that our legislators could have committed so gross an act of injustice and intolerance."
>
> "Then the blacks possess the right of voting in this country?"
>
> "Without doubt."
>
> "How comes it, then, that at the polling-booth this morning I did not perceive a single Negro?"

"That is not the fault of the law. The Negroes have an undisputed right of voting, but they voluntarily abstain from making their appearance."

"A very pretty piece of modesty on their part!" rejoined I.

"Why, the truth is that they are not disinclined to vote, but they are afraid of being maltreated; in this country the law is sometimes unable to maintain its authority without the support of the majority. But in this case the majority entertains very strong prejudices against the blacks, and the magistrates are unable to protect them in the exercise of their legal rights."

"Then the majority claims the right not only of making the laws, but of breaking the laws it has made?"[6]

Tocqueville also offers this prophetic insight thirty years before our Civil War: "If ever America undergoes great revolutions, they will be brought about by the presence of the black race on the soil of the United States; that is to say, they will owe their origin, not to the equality, but to the inequality of condition."[7]

In many ways our vision and conduct have improved. For African Americans, we have moved from the days of abolishing slavery—at least on paper—to legal segregation, and then to a society with many more opportunities for minorities. Progress usually has been slow. The Constitution banned the sea traffic in slavery beginning in 1808, twenty years after the ratification of the Constitution. Gradually other steps took place, and occasionally negative actions such as the 1896 Supreme Court decision legalizing segregation were taken. But the overall direction was positive. Have we completely rid our soil of racism? Unfortunately, we know the answer to that. In 1829, David Walker, a free black man living in Boston, wrote a pamphlet attacking slavery and included this comment: "It pleased [God] to make us black—which color Mr. Jefferson calls unfortunate! As though we are not as thankful to our God, for having made us as it pleased Himself, as they [the whites] are for having made them white."[8] Yet in 2002, Carol Moseley-Braun, the first African American woman to serve as a U.S. senator, wrote: "I have to come to grips with the stark reality that the skin I am in makes me the least powerful, the least respected, the least valued of all of God's children on this earth."[9]

Native Americans often found themselves cruelly mistreated at the hands of the Western European invaders of their land. In 1838, for example, twenty-six years after having fought with General Andrew Jackson in the War of 1812, the Cherokees were forced by then-President Jackson to move from the Southeast to Oklahoma, Kansas, and Nebraska. Sixteen thousand made the march; four thousand died along the way. It became known as the Trail of Tears. Native Americans still remain at the bottom of most economic and social statistical analyses of ethnic groups in our country, whether the measure is income or unemployment or alcoholism. Indifference to their plight by most Americans has compounded all the difficulties. But their opportunities have improved as a result of schools created under the Tribally Controlled Community Colleges Act, as well as other undramatic developments, along with tribally sponsored gambling casinos, which are at best a mixed blessing to the Indians and the rest of the population.

Women did not have the right to vote, and in many states they could not testify in court or own property. Most job opportunities were denied them. In my lifetime I have seen the career choices for women open in almost every field—yet substantial barriers remain. When he ran for reelection to the Illinois House of Representatives in 1836, young Abraham Lincoln advocated women's suffrage—almost a century before the federal government acted on that—but there is no record of Lincoln ever mentioning it again. My guess is that he received so much adverse comment from the male voters that he decided no early victory was achievable on that front.

During World War I, a leader in the effort to achieve the right to vote for women had a widely distributed tongue-in-cheek folder titled "Why We Oppose Votes for Men." The reasons included these, ordinarily used in reverse:

> Because men will lose their charm if they step out of their natural sphere and interest themselves in other matters than feats of arms, uniforms and drums.
>
> Because men are too emotional to vote. Their conduct at baseball games and political conventions shows this, while their innate tendency to appeal to force renders them particularly unfit for the task of government.[10]

We denied Asian Americans the opportunity for citizenship and in California even the right to own property. Railroad barons imported Chinese in large numbers to build our railroads. Asian Americans for decades were limited to vegetable farming, running laundries or restaurants, or doing the most menial work. Today Asian Americans play increasingly important roles, not only as engineers and physicians, but more and more in other leadership positions. However, prejudices persist.

Latino Americans—now our largest minority—played a key part in the development of the Southwest and, after decades of being largely ignored, are playing a more visible part in political leadership in many states, in addition to emerging as leaders in the arts and other fields. Their role will grow enormously, as studies of population and economic trends show. But serious difficulties remain, including the inexcusable sub-standard treatment of Americans on the island of Puerto Rico. "Commonwealth status" is a nice-sounding phrase that hides old-fashioned colonialism that treats people as second-class citizens even though they serve in our armed forces and perform other tasks we expect of first-class citizens.

The anti-Catholicism and anti-Semitism all too prevalent even in my lifetime have largely disappeared, but not totally. The negative stereotypes of Muslims and Arabs were much too slowly diminishing, but in the aftermath of September 11th there is a mixed pattern of greater sensitivity and understanding by many, and greater hostility and uninformed prejudice by others.

While people with disabilities now have a much greater opportunity for education and employment, they still have difficulty in obtaining positions they are capable of handling.

We speak more frankly about the problems that gay men and lesbians face, a necessary first step toward equal treatment.

That list goes on. Romani (Gypsies) face discrimination. Overweight people sometimes do. Often older people find the door of opportunity shut.

Our stated vision is clear: "All men are created equal..." Our practice is frequently less clear.

It took 139 years from Washington's first day as president until a political party nominated a Roman Catholic, Governor Alfred Smith of New York, who lost his Democratic race for president to Republican Herbert Hoover, many crediting Smith's defeat to the virulent anti-Catholicism that haunted the nation from its earliest days. Thirty-two years later, John F. Kennedy ran for president and in most areas of the nation the big question discussed was, "Can we survive as a democracy if we elect a Roman Catholic as president?" Today it is hard to believe that could have been an issue. Those who took the anti-Catholic stance noted that most of the plentiful supply of dictators in Latin America were Roman Catholics. Conscientious and concerned non-Catholics were joined by demagogues in stirring fears of this "foreign" religion. Kennedy won by a slim margin and his performance, plus the moderating moves of Pope John XXIII and Vatican Council II, combined to kill that form of prejudice for almost all people in our nation. By the year 2000, when the Democratic party picked Senator Joseph Lieberman, a practicing Jew, as its candidate for vice president, his religion was a non-issue. Thirty years earlier—certainly fifty years earlier—that would have stirred a major national debate. Abraham Foxman, director of the Anti-Defamation League, noted that "approximately 12 percent of the American people have strong anti-Semitic views [but] these people don't vote anyway."[11] There's good news and bad news in that statement issued in the year 2000. Two years later the Anti-Defamation League reported that "unquestionably anti-Semitic" views had risen to 17 percent, undoubtedly aggravated by the Middle East conflict.[12]

The first American political party to hold a national convention was the Anti-Masonic Party in 1831. Even though George Washington held membership in that fraternal group, prejudice ran high (as it still does in a few European nations) and rumors about the Masons' secret oaths generated fears. When reports spread that a bricklayer in New York had been killed for violating his oath of secrecy, that inflamed the not-so-latent anti-Masonic prejudices. Anti-Masonic newspapers emerged, and a national convention of the Anti-Masonic political party met in Baltimore. They carried only Vermont, which then had seven electoral votes. When calm prevailed and the anti-Masonic winds subsided, the political party disappeared.

The United States also had an entity that called itself the American Party, based on secret lodges in most of the larger cities of the nation, with local groups known as the Order of the Star-Spangled Banner. When members were asked what the group did, the order instructed them to respond, "I know nothing." The public labeled them the Know-Nothing Party. Their strong anti-Catholic, anti-Jewish, and anti-immigrant views—particularly opposing Irish and German immigration—had temporary emotional appeal. In the first half of the nineteenth century strong protests—sometimes violent—erupted against the Irish and Germans. In part it reflected the strong anti-Catholic sentiment of that period. At one point none of the colonies—not even Maryland—would permit Catholics to vote. The Irish and Germans, generally poorly educated people who gathered in impoverished neighborhoods, became the subjects of rumors that had no substance. A former mayor of New York City, Philip Hone, described the Irish and Germans as "filthy, intemperate, unused to the comforts of life" and having no regard for the proprieties of dealing with other people. "Not one in twenty is competent to keep himself."[13] Politics then—as politics now—sometimes had an emotional anti-immigrant orientation. In 1852 the Know-Nothings elected forty-three members of Congress. Four years later they dropped dramatically as a political force.

Before that happened—and seven years before he became president—Abraham Lincoln wrote to his friend Joshua Speed:

> I am not a Know-Nothing. That is certain. How could I be? How can anyone who abhors the oppression of negroes be in favor of degrading classes of white people? Our progress in degeneracy appears to me to be pretty rapid. As a nation, we began by declaring that "all men are created equal." We now practically read it "all men are created equal, except negroes." When the Know-Nothings get control, it will read "all men are created equal, except negroes, and foreigners and catholics." When it comes to this I should prefer emigrating to some country where they make no pretense of loving liberty—in Russia, for instance where despotism can be taken pure, and without the base alloy of hypocrisy.[14]

The anti-immigrant sentiment in the nation waxes and wanes. There is always some hostility toward the latest group of immigrants —hostility born out of ignorance and fear—and the strong feeling that "they" won't fit into our American culture. During World War I patriotism somehow became enmeshed with not speaking and teaching another language, particularly German. Schools and churches and synagogues that served non-English speaking ethnic populations awkwardly moved into the English language to prove to the sometimes hysterical population that they were truly American. But isolated incidents of aroused and misdirected public passion sullied our record of protecting the rights of all citizens. In Collinsville, Illinois, for example, word spread that a coal miner, Robert Prager, a German immigrant who could not speak

English, was a spy. No one asked the obvious question: How could a coal miner who could not speak English do any good for Germany as a spy? But reason did not prevail, and despite the efforts to protect him in the local jail, a mob grabbed him and hanged him.

In February 1942, President Franklin D. Roosevelt ordered 115,000 Japanese Americans in California, Oregon, and Washington to sell everything they owned in as little as three days, pack everything into one suitcase, and be taken off to camps in the interior of the nation. This number included many who wanted to become citizens but could not because of our discriminatory laws. There was no evidence of espionage. We were perpetrating a terrible and clear violation of their rights—but the action had overwhelming popularity, largely because of the attack by the Japanese on Pearl Harbor three months earlier, and also in part because of racism, which the Japanese military assault escalated. The action and subsequent unusual behavior of respected leaders became a matter of national embarrassment in later years. The head of the FBI, J. Edgar Hoover, later insensitive on civil liberties, opposed the president's action. The Supreme Court ruled 6-3 in the Korematsu decision that President Roosevelt had the right to take the action. The decision was written by Justice Hugo Black and concurred in by Justice William Douglas, both later strong champions of basic freedoms. Roger Baldwin, head of the American Civil Liberties Union (ACLU), sharply criticized the president's action. Shortly after that, the national board of the ACLU held an emergency meeting and by a 2-1 vote backed the president and not Roger Baldwin. Urging the president to take the action was California Attorney General Earl Warren, later chief justice of the U. S. Supreme Court and a champion of civil rights. A strange episode in our nation's history, it remains a sharp reminder that good intentions at a time of fervent patriotism can lead to bad results.

Our experience after September 11th is no exception. We must make sure that one of the victims of the somewhat misnamed "war on terrorism" is not the Bill of Rights of the U. S. Constitution.

10

California's Proposition 187, which passed in a referendum there in 1994, aimed at restricting the rights of immigrants. Efforts to have "English as the official language" are a slightly more sophisticated anti-immigrant endeavor that manages to enlist many people who are not opposed to the new citizens. The reality is that we have a higher percentage of our citizens whose mother tongue is English today than we did fifty years ago or one hundred years ago. And, ironically, many legislators who get on the anti-foreign language bandwagon vote against appropriations to teach people English as a second language. In many urban areas there is a waiting list to get into such courses. Hostility to immigrants is part of our history, but fortunately the immigrant haters generally don't prevail.

Over and over and over again the nation has been enriched by immigrants, and almost all of us are the heirs of immigrants. We do have a problem with *illegal* immigration, a problem relatively easily solved (on paper) by placing a heavier penalty on employers who knowingly hire people who are not here legally. Jobs that pay more here than in other countries are the major magnet that draws undocumented people. Former senator Alan Simpson, a Republican from Wyoming, Senator Ted Kennedy, a Democrat from Massachusetts, and I tried to strengthen the penalty provisions of the law but ran into strong opposition from the Restaurant Association, the Farm Bureau, the Manufacturers Association, and the Chamber of Commerce. They prevailed. We have more *legal* immigration—in numbers—into this country than the rest of the world combined and it is a great asset to us. In percentage terms, a few other nations do better, and we are not as generous as a handful of other countries in admitting refugees. In 2002, the United States admitted only thirty thousand refugees, the lowest number in twenty-five years. Our Social Security Retirement Fund faces serious problems, but not as serious as those faced by several other industrial nations. The principal reason for our better status is that we have had a steady influx of immigrants who pay into the system and in many cases return to their home country before drawing any Social Security retirement benefits.

Our boast of equality ought to include fairness to those who immigrate to this country legally. In one of the punitive sections of the immigration act passed in 1996, people who entered this nation legally were denied access to food stamps if they became desperate. This passed well before September 11, 2001, when Father Robert McChesney, head of the immigration and refugee service for the Jesuits in Los Angeles, noted that "unscrupulous elements of the press found increasing profit in sensationalizing a story of immigrant hordes and terrorists breaching permeable borders to attack the fabric of American society."[15] The measure hit Congress when fear and fervor were at fever pitch. Only three of us voted against it. Since September 11th the fears have intensified and the fervor has not lessened, resulting in civil liberties abuses.

The public impression today is that most illegal aliens come from Mexico. While the Mexican numbers are large, they do not compose the majority. The bulk of those here illegally came from other nations on visitors' visas, student visas, or some other legal category and then stayed when they legally should have left.

We have yet to work out sensible, cooperative arrangements with Mexico on immigration. The North America Free Trade Agreement (NAFTA) between Canada, Mexico, and the United States, which many predicted would do great harm to our nation, has helped all three countries measurably. Since its enactment, 1.6 million Mexicans have moved above the poverty line, lessening somewhat the pressures for illegal crossing of the U.S.-Mexican border.

A year-end economic summary in December 2002 noted: "Since 1993, manufacturing output in the United States has risen at an annual rate of 3.7 percent, 50 percent faster than during the eight years before the enactment of NAFTA. The number of manufacturing jobs grew by 700,000 in the first four years of NAFTA."[16] The Ross Perot prediction in the presidential debates that we would "hear a giant sucking sound of jobs being pulled out of this country"[17] turned out to be false, as almost all anti-free trade speeches have through the years.

In the immigration and trade arenas, it is easy to prey on fears that we have to watch out for "those people" taking away our jobs. Fortunately, the fear-mongers have generally not prevailed in the two-plus centuries of our existence as a nation. Economist George Gilder points out that immigrants have been responsible for "a spate of inventions and technical advances, from microwaves and air bags to digital cable and satellite television, from home computers and air conditioners to cellular phones and lifesaving pharmaceutical and medical devices." He estimates that without immigration over the five recent decades, U.S. living standards would be "at least 40 percent lower."[18]

In sheer numbers, we have admitted more immigrants into the United States than ever before, but that distorts the reality. We now admit annually roughly 4 immigrants for every 1,000 American citizens. A century ago, in the decade 1901 to 1910, we admitted 10.4 per 1,000 citizens. Approximately 10 percent of our population today is foreign born; a century ago it was 14.7 percent.

For several years I served as publisher of a small weekly newspaper in a rural community, Troy, Illinois, a town that up until that time had neither African Americans nor Jews—and unfortunately took pride in that fact. I employed Charles Klotzer, whose trail as a Jew took him from Nazi Germany to Shanghai and eventually to the United States. He did a great job at my newspaper and later founded the *St. Louis Journalism Review* and a typesetting company. No one can convince me that we would be a better nation without Charles Klotzer.

The Luddites of the nineteenth century opposed machinery. The Luddites of today oppose immigration.

THE AMERICAN DREAM will always be partially unfulfilled. No nation, no religious group, no individual completely lives up to professed ideals. But when the nation's leaders appeal to the noble in us, we can rise to unexpected heights. That is true also beyond our borders. When President Anwar Sadat of Egypt took the dramatic step of visiting the Israeli Knesset (parliament), he startled his people and Arab leaders in other nations. Many Arab dignitaries predicted that he would not survive twenty-four hours when he returned to Egypt. But President Sadat went back, rode in an open Cadillac, and millions cheered him in the streets of Cairo. He called upon their better instincts and they responded. Yes, a few years later extremists assassinated him, but their bullets did not scar his image as one of the giants of the twentieth century.

Particularly in times of national emergency, people in all nations tend to rally around their leadership, whether that leadership is good or bad. During times of emergency there is also an unfortunate tendency to trample on basic civil liberties.

We are likely to look back on our post-September 11th Justice Department actions with regret. Arguing that an American-born detainee is not entitled to see a lawyer will not look good twenty years from now. At Guantanamo Base in Cuba, we held twelve hundred people for months, most of whom had apparently fought for the Taliban. We did not make known their names or countries of origin or provide any counsel, conduct beneath our nation's standards. As of this writing the number held there is over six hundred, with no improvement in their rights or in information. If Saddam Hussein had done this, we would rightfully and indignantly denounce him. To believe that people around the world will assume that our motives are pure and that we do not have to follow certain basic humanitarian minimums as outlined in the Geneva Convention is to court lowered international prestige and cooperation.

After the terrorist attack, Attorney General John Ashcroft announced that we would have military tribunals—used only in the Civil War and in one case during World War II—for suspected terrorists. These would not be military trials like those who serve in our armed forces receive, trials where the accused have access to the records and choose their lawyers, but secret trials that can order the death penalty, where the defendants cannot see the evidence against them and cannot choose their lawyers. However, more than a year after announcing that there would be military tribunals, none has taken place and it may be that more thoughtful views have prevailed.

One year after the September 11th disaster, the United States is slowing almost to a standstill in processing visa applications from tens of thousands of Muslim men who wish to enter the United States temporarily or permanently. Most are university students. If the United States wants to slow all visa applications to have them checked by the FBI and the CIA, that would be constitutional. But to select men on the basis of their religious belief is clearly in violation of the spirit and letter of the Constitution, though the Supreme Court has yet to rule on this. Unfortunately, the Court has a history of sometimes being caught up in the fervor of the times during national crises, doing what is popular, then years later reversing itself. One news account says that the visa delays are "disrupting lives, creating diplomatic tensions and causing headaches for American diplomats.... One American official said there was a backlog of [at] least 100,000 visa applications now being reviewed by the FBI and CIA."[19] In addition to students, Muslim business leaders and others are being denied timely visas to attend meetings in the United States. One U.S. ambassador is quoted as saying that this is creating ill will when we need good will. The foreign minister of Pakistan, whose government went out of its way at substantial domestic risk to help the U.S. after September 11th, complained that students and visitors from Pakistan were being treated unfairly by our Immigration Service—not a good way to say thanks for their help.

The Constitution does not permit us to pass laws that discriminate on the basis of creed or race or ethnic background. It may seem convenient from time to time to ignore the Constitution, but such conduct jeopardizes our free future—and also creates adversaries in the Muslim world when we need friends. One of the victims of the "war on terrorism" should not be our basic civil liberties. When the Justice Department announces that thousands of immigrants from Arab countries will be questioned "voluntarily" by the FBI and local police, that sends chills into more than Arab

Americans. When a routine FBI question is "Do you pray five times a day?" that violates our First Amendment.

WE HAVE GRADUALLY BECOME more sensitive to our basic rights, which are the hallmark of freedom. But we seem to need to learn that lesson over and over.

In 1798 it looked as if the youthful United States government was headed for war with France, a nation that had helped us gain independence from the British, but was now led by the adventurous Napoleon Bonaparte. In the fervor of the moment, Congress passed the Alien and Sedition Acts, which authorized President John Adams to deport any alien the government deemed to be dangerous and included a sweeping prohibition against publication of "false or malicious writings" about the federal government. Two years later, when it became clear that no war threatened us, Congress repealed the measures and President Thomas Jefferson—to whom French visitor-observer Alexis de Tocqueville referred in 1831 as "the most powerful advocate democracy has ever had"[20]—signed the repeal.

AFTER WORLD WAR II, when a belligerent Soviet Union led by Joseph Stalin attempted to subvert governments in developing nations, Senator Joseph McCarthy of Wisconsin made unfounded charges that people in key positions in the federal government were Communists and loyal to the Soviets rather than to our government. He also made loose charges about books being Communist-tinged. Super-patriots demanded that textbooks be changed and that other books be removed from libraries, including libraries the United States had sponsored in Germany during the years immediately after World War II. We had properly criticized Hitler for burning books, and yet we found ourselves in the embarrassing situation of removing books from libraries because of their content, thanks to public pressure galvanized by one senator.

The danger that in moments of a national crisis we will abandon basic safeguards of our liberties will always exist. Such moments require a few people of courage to be champions of liberty.

Fortunately, we have had champions of liberty before the infringements of our constitutional rights endured lengthy abuse. Sometimes those champions endured temporary unpopularity, as Martin Luther King Jr. did in fighting segregation in the South, or President Harry Truman did in issuing his executive order ending segregation in the military. That courageous action, opposed by many of our military leaders, took the nation by surprise. The next day President Truman appeared before a joint session of Congress and his reception was "noticeably cool."[21] When a president enters to address Congress, the long tradition is that all members rise to pay respect, no matter how much they may disagree with him. On this occasion, some members did not rise as the president entered. The applause of history is on the side of those who are defenders of human rights.

Numerically the biggest human rights problem we have had in our nation is the unfair treatment of African Americans. The abuse of Native Americans has been shameful, and other groups—including Catholics, Jews, Mormons, Asian Americans, and gays—have faced serious difficulties. Our costliest war centered on the slavery issue. Since that war, brutal and crude segregation laws in the South had their counterpart in segregation and discrimination practices in the North. The national conscience gradually became aroused, thanks particularly to Martin Luther King Jr. The sweeping Civil Rights Act of 1964 would not have passed without his eloquent voice and the leadership of Senator Paul Douglas of Illinois and a convert to the cause, President Lyndon Johnson. Public opinion polls showed a majority of whites indifferent to the discrimination, despite clarion calls for justice by most major religious leaders. Of his Democratic colleagues in the Senate, Paul Douglas wrote to his wife: "One difficulty we have is that while most of our people care about civil rights, they don't care deeply."[22] Every noble but controversial cause needs at least one bulldog to battle ceaselessly for its success in a legislative body. Then, years later, the public looks back and wonders why the measure didn't pass easily.

Temporary unpopularity is sometimes reversed quickly if the public senses that a leader's motivation is good. There is a yearning for leaders we can trust who will appeal to the best in us, who will help us build a more sensitive and just society and world.

In a speech two years before his election as president, Abraham Lincoln said:

> What constitutes the bulwark of our own liberty and independence? It is not our frowning battlements, our bristling sea coasts, the guns of our war steamers, or the strength of our gallant and disciplined army. These are not our reliance against a resumption of tyranny in our fair land. All of them may be turned against our liberties, without making us stronger or weaker for the struggle. Our reliance is in the love of liberty which God has planted in our bosoms. Our defense is in the preservation of the spirit which prizes liberty as the heritage of all men, in all lands, everywhere.[23]

Lincoln, it should be added, felt compelled to suspend habeas corpus —one of our basic civil liberties protections—but considering the nature of the nation's most difficult struggle, he showed remarkable restraint.

David Christensen, a retired faculty member at Southern Illinois University, favors changing the Pledge of Allegiance from "with liberty and justice for all" to "striving for liberty and justice for all." I like that touch of reality. All of us can do more to make those words live. Each of us can place a small piece in the mosaic of equality and freedom and a more civilized society.

CHAPTER TWO

RELIGION

Men will wrangle for religion; write for it; fight for it; die for it, anything but—live for it.

—C. C. Colton, 1820[1]

In terms of religion, our nation does not fit into a predictable mold.

Our Declaration of Independence mentions God four times. Our Constitution does not mention God.

Despite the fact that nine of the thirteen colonies had some type of official tie with a church denomination, the authors of our Constitution called for no established religion. This made us, at one point, unique among the nations of the world. Yet by beliefs expressed in polls, or attendance at religious services, we are among the most religious of the world's people.

Religion played a dominant role in the lives of the Puritans and many other early immigrants, both in the cause of their coming here and in the laws they made. The colony of Connecticut for example, had as the preamble to its legal code: "Whoever shall worship any God other than the Lord shall surely be put to death."[2] This was followed by other specific biblically based reasons for the death penalty: blasphemy, sorcery, adultery, rape, and choosing to worship God in a differing ritual. However, death as a punishment rarely occurred. The penal code of the Massachusetts colony called for the death penalty for a Catholic priest who returned to Massachusetts after having been banished from it.[3] Massachusetts law also called for execution if a Quaker, banished from the colony, returned. In 1649 four Quakers, including a woman, Mary Dyer, received the death penalty. Early Baptist leader Roger Williams founded the colony of Rhode Island and championed religious freedom after facing the prospect of persecution in Massachusetts for his beliefs. Religious rigidity and religious prejudice, so dominant in the early years of the colonies, gradually diminished. The reaction to those harsh early statutes was so profound that the experiment of not having an established church became part of the nation, along with full freedom of worship. By the year 1831, Tocqueville could visit the United States and marvel at the freedom religious leaders had and their influence for good. He noted: "A certain number of Americans pursue a peculiar form of worship from habit more than conviction ... but there is no country in the world where the Christian religion retains a greater influence over the souls of men than in America.... Despotism may govern without faith, but liberty cannot."[4]

He also observed: "In France I had almost always seen the spirit of religion and the spirit of freedom marching in opposite directions. But in America I found they were intimately united.... My desire to discover the causes of this phenomenon increased from day to day.... I questioned the clergy of all the different sects. ... To each of these men I expressed my astonishment.... They all attributed the peaceful dominion of religion in their country mainly to the separation of church and state."[5]

Today we are a diverse nation in our ethnic backgrounds, and probably *the* most diverse country in our religious heritage. In both ethnic and religious affiliation, there is frequently a grand mixing. Forrest Church, son of former Idaho senator Frank Church and pastor of All Souls Unitarian Church in New York City, tells of his background:

On my father's side the first member of my family to come here...came to Boston in 1630, and was a founder of the First Church in Boston....He was a Puritan who came to escape religious persecution in England....On my mother's side one of the first ancestors to go all the way West [was] a fellow who came from Scotland and went across the country with Brigham Young and became a Mormon bishop in Utah. My grandfather was a Quaker, as well as a judge, and he would never sit on a case where there would be the possibility of capital punishment, because his religion would not allow him to make that sentence....My wife's ancestors [were] Jews from Germany who came over here and intermarried with Catholics and Presbyterians.[6]

He somehow missed Baptists and Lutherans and Muslims and others. But most Americans represent a religious diversity, either through their family heritage or because that diversity has quietly seeped into our cultural sensitivity.

For many early immigrants, one of the appeals of coming to our nation was religious freedom. One group of 612 from Germany, for example, signed a statement in the 1830s complaining of their inability to practice their faith in the Dresden and Saxony area and seeking a place where they could worship freely. Their statement concludes: "Such a country...is the United States...for there, as nowhere else in the world, perfect religious and civil liberty prevails."[7]

If the polls are to be believed, Americans strongly support a separation of church and state, yet when an appellate court rules that the insertion of the words "under God" in the Pledge of Allegiance goes too far in mixing church and state, 90 percent of the population disagree with that decision. (Interestingly, when Lincoln delivered his Gettysburg Address, he extemporaneously inserted the words "under God," not part of his prepared text.)

Our inconsistencies are legion. While many complain that American individualism and secular influences have resulted in a privatization of faith so that people seldom see their religious moorings related to politics or economics, others protest that zealots are trying to make ours "a Christian nation" which follows the dogmas of that faith and is intolerant of other beliefs or non-belief. They point to everything from the early burning of "witches" to current efforts to dictate to schools what can be taught about the beginnings of our planet.

My own non-theologian's view of religion is that when it evokes a meanness of spirit, it is flawed; that is a distortion of faith. The non-listening vehement I'm-right-and-you're-wrong attitude—and emotional displays—too easily lead to an I'm-good-and-you're-bad attitude and that can lead to extremes which erupt in violence.

Twice in recent days on my car radio I have picked up a network call-in host, Neal Boortz, who is passionate in his denunciation of Muslims and their conduct. I am sure what he says appeals to the ego of his largely Christian and somewhat smaller Jewish audience. But it is demagoguery. He fails to point out that Christians and Jews also have a history in which extremists and even major leaders have caused bloodshed on a massive scale. The selective view of current events and history which glorifies us and vilifies others is a great disservice to truth, to future generations, and to ourselves. It causes us to make decisions by viewing events through a distorted lens.

We tend to be selective in our views of history and current events, and we are also selective in what we stress in our own beliefs. I agree totally with those who decry the sentence of stoning to death of a woman caught in adultery in the Muslim region of Nigeria (a sentence not carried out), but the Hebrew and Christian scriptures call for the same. We will never know how many hundreds of thousands of Muslims and Jews suffered brutal deaths at the hands of Christians during the crusades. Conservative Christian groups cite the book of Deuteronomy and its "life for life, eye for eye, tooth for tooth" admonition as mandating capital punishment. Ignored parts of the same scriptural book call for stoning to death anyone who converts to another religion and slaying men, women, and children when a territory is conquered: "In the cities ... the Lord your God gives you ... you shall save alive nothing that breathes" (Deuteronomy 20:16). And, among other offenses, a rebellious son in a family should be stoned to death. If applied today, that might result in a shortage of stones! Another command in the same book of Hebrew and Christian scriptures that I have not seen followed: "When men fight with one another, and the wife of the one draws near to rescue her husband from the hand of him who is beating him, and puts out her hand and seizes him by his private parts, then you shall cut off her hand" (Deuteronomy 25:11). The slaying of heretics in the early history of New England was not carried out by Muslims. The people killing each other in Northern Ireland are not Muslims. Strange stands and actions are evident in every faith.

Only one of the thirteen colonies, Rhode Island, permitted Quakers to reside within its borders.

Jerry Falwell's "Moral Majority"—may it rest in peace—one year gave me a zero rating on moral issues before Congress. One of my "immoral" acts: voting for foreign aid, the government program that over the years has prevented millions from starving to death or dying prematurely.

Statements by a few fundamentalist U.S. Christian leaders that Muslims are "worse than the Nazis," that Islam is "a very evil and wicked religion," that Muhammad was "a demon-possessed pedophile" receive wide circulation in Muslim nations and are valuable tools in the hands of those who want to build an anti-U.S. public relations base.[8] A new, widely distributed brochure comments: "Islam is at war with the Christian West.... As recently as 1683, the armies of Islam were besieging Vienna.... Islam is, quite simply, a religion of war.... There is no such thing as peaceful or tolerant Islam."[9] More public relations fodder for Muslim extremists! One of the co-authors of that distortion wrote an article in 1999 suggesting that the nation would have been better off if the South had won the Civil War.[10]

Only a few decades ago, Protestants in the U.S. were still making extreme statements about Roman Catholics. Not only were the early colonies militantly anti-Catholic, the pamphlet advocating independence and widely distributed in January and February 1776 written by Thomas Paine, "Common Sense," contains the phrase "*jesuitically* adopted by the king [George III] and his parasites, with a low *papistical* design" (italics mine).[11] In 1835, a widely circulated pamphlet written by Samuel F. B. Morse—who nine years later was to invent the telegraph—was titled, "The Dangers of Popery." He wrote about Catholicism organizing for our free elections even though it "cannot from its nature tolerate any of those civil rights which are the peculiar boast of Americans."[12] While his pamphlet did not advocate violence, it resulted in riots and bloodshed. In 1960—prior to Vatican II—I married Jeanne Hurley, a Roman Catholic. Both of us were state legislators and in the public eye. Those were the days when engagements usually were announced before marriages. After that announcement, I was amazed at the bitterness that some people had toward the son and brother of a Lutheran minister marrying a good Roman Catholic and to an active Catholic woman marrying a Lutheran.

A century ago both Protestants and Catholics thought Mormons to be a huge, subversive threat to our nation. In 1903 Utah elected a Mormon to the United States Senate and for three years that body refused to permanently seat him. The Senate Judiciary Committee voted seven to five not to seat him.

No religion should be judged by its extremists, and those who spread hate and fear in the name of religion hurt their own faith as much as they distort the beliefs of others.

This does not preclude candor in speaking to people of differing beliefs, a candor that too often is lacking. Getting together in "feel good" sessions where honest differences are not discussed is better than not getting together, but something more needs to be built on that base. Muslims from other nations, for example, find our practice of separating religion from the state confusing. Some view it as state atheism. Muslim adjustments over the centuries have come through gradual evolution, not with sudden jolts like our Reformation and Vatican II. Nicholas Kristof of the *New York*

Times is not excessively confrontational when he writes: "If Muslim countries are to modernize, they must update traditional religious doctrines about punishment [and] the role of women."[13] The reality is that most Muslim nations, like most Christian nations, have abandoned the harshest of their ancient rules. Kristof's column was written from Sudan, a nation vastly different in its practices from Jordan or Morocco or Tunisia or Turkey or Bangladesh. But Muslims can improve their practices, and the rest of us can also.

Greater freedom for their people will help Muslim nations economically and intellectually. A report for the United Nations in 2002 by several Arab Muslim intellectual leaders—primarily from Saudi Arabia and Egypt—notes "a severe shortage of new and stimulating writing" and adds that "the whole Arab world translates about 300 books annually, one-fifth the number that Greece does." The number of Arab translations of books is woefully deficient, the report states. "The Arabs have translated as many books in 1,000 years as Spain translates in just one year."[14]

There are deficiencies—and worse—in the history and performance of every faith group.

Seven weeks after September 11th, while the U.S. military and media focused on efforts in Afghanistan, the Jesuit publication, *America*, concluded its editorial with this accurate summation: "This war will not be won in the mountains of Afghanistan. It will be won when Muslims are convinced that the United States acts justly."[15] The U.S., in its desire to corner Osama bin Laden and his followers, bombed much of Afghanistan. But humanitarian follow-through has been more limited. During the eighteen months following the war, international aid has not built a single new home in the capital city of Kabul, which has three million people. Huge numbers live in tents in this desperately cold city six thousand feet above sea level.[16]

WE LEARN TO *tolerate* pain when we go to the dentist; we *tolerate* the noise the neighbors make; we may *tolerate* the taste of mushrooms or green peppers or aspirin. We generally speak about tolerating what we dislike.

But there is another meaning, a more noble tilt to the word. Tolerance can also mean that we respect the beliefs or culture of other groups even if we do not join in their culture or beliefs. This type of tolerance also implies that we *listen* to others. We can enrich ourselves by listening. Tolerance and understanding do not imply that all political or religious beliefs are equal in validity, but they lead us away from an excessive and sometimes violent zealotry.

I do not have to accept the full beliefs of Christian Scientists to recognize the truth of their stress on the unreality of many "illnesses" and health complaints. Certain maladies are often in the mind; they frequently are functional rather than organic in nature. Whether or not I accept all beliefs of Christian Scientists, the fact that I listen and learn from them is helpful to me and helpful in creating a cohesive society.

Real listening also suggests an openness to the possibility of accepting at least some of the views of another person. Rigidity of opinion and listening do not go together. Former senator Alan Simpson observed: "We must deal with sick people of all races and creeds who are true believers. I always have had a lot of trouble with 100 percent-ers. Show me a 100 percent-er and I will show you someone I want to stay away from."[17]

I once found myself in an unusual situation. Scheduled to speak in a community near mine was a leader of a group that called itself America First, headed by a bigot named Gerald L. K. Smith, who noisily condemned Catholics, Jews, African Americans (then called Negroes), immigrants, and others. I believed in nothing the group stood for, but the sheriff of our county announced that he would not let Smith's follower speak. I called the sheriff and told him that the sheriff's responsibility was to defend that person's right to speak. The man finally gave his talk. Thirteen people showed up and the public quickly forgot the whole matter. If the sheriff had stopped him, the speaker and his followers would have portrayed themselves as martyrs and eventually would have had a much bigger crowd after the courts had inevitably ruled that he had a right to express his views.

Building understanding between Muslims and the Christian and Jewish communities is now more visibly important. Muslims point—with accuracy—to bloody, violent attacks on followers of Islam by Christians and Jews. Christians and Jews note violent action by Muslims—with accuracy. A small incident that took place in 1786 takes on added interest because of the September 11th terrorist attacks. John Adams, in London on a diplomatic mission for our new nation, by chance visited with the Sultan of Tripoli, who expressed serious concern about the lack of diplomatic relations between the United States and Tripoli, a situation that could be strained to the point of war. Historian David McCullough notes the Sultan's observations: "A war between Christian and Christian was mild, prisoners were treated with humanity; but, warned His Excellency, a war between Muslim and Christian could be horrible."[18]

It is strange but true that religion can be a factor for greater cruelty rather than for amelioration of a conflict. There are people in all camps who are spiritually deaf, who can only view any situation through the warped lens of extremists of their faith and never really listen to others. They are piling logs on the fires of violence. Princeton religion professor Elaine Pagels says: "Practically no religion...sees other people in a way that affirms the others' choices."[19] When Pope John Paul II visited South Carolina in 1987, Bob Jones Jr., chancellor of Bob Jones University, did no one a service by saying he "would as soon speak to the devil himself" as to the Pope.[20] Religion should be a force for healing, and when it is used as a cloak to hide hatred, the person using that cloak is doing a great disservice to the faith that he or she professes.

The U.S. Army stationed me in Germany shortly after World War II. It was an important experience for me. When conversation with local Germans veered in the direction of the Holocaust and Christian-Jewish relations, one of the stories I heard told of a pastor who knuckled under to Hitler. At the beginning of the Sunday morning service he said, "Will anyone who has any Jewish blood please leave this service immediately." No one moved. He repeated his request, and the Christ on the crucifix came down off the cross and walked out of the church. Not a true story, of course, but its moral is true.

When extremists who are Christian or Jewish or Muslim or of any faith or of no faith preach hatred, they reinforce the terrorists they profess to oppose. The world has experienced too much of this.

After September 11th, many of us anticipated that there would be a host of acts of hatred and violence against Muslims. There were more than we would have liked, but fewer than many of us expected. A 2002 civil rights report by the Council on American Islamic Relations noted that anti-Muslim incidents increased 43 percent over the year 2001. A problem present before September 11th grew, but it did not multiply as much as many of us feared it would. In some communities, Christians and Jews literally joined hands around mosques to protect Muslim worshipers who had received hate messages.

Tolerance grows out of knowledge, and knowledge grows out of tolerance. We do not tolerate something we fear, something we know little about, something that someone has distorted. It is no accident that the higher the level of education, the less likely a person is to have prejudices and stereotypes of people of other races, religions, ethnic groups, sexual orientation, and nationalities.

Sixteen-year-old Amy Maddox of Bargersville, Indiana, wrote the following poem:

> He prayed—it wasn't my religion.
> He ate—it wasn't what I ate.
> He spoke—it wasn't my language.
> He dressed—it wasn't what I wore.
> He took my hand—it wasn't the color of mine.
> But when he laughed—it was

how I laughed, and when he cried–
it was how I cried.[21]

MORE THAN IN MOST democracies, in the U.S. candidates for high public office frequently parade their religion. As governor of Texas, George W. Bush declared "Jesus Day" on June 10th of the year of his presidential race, and in response to a question during that campaign said his favorite philosopher was Jesus. Vice President Al Gore Jr. said he often asks himself, "What would Jesus do?" It is difficult to know when religion is being abused, and when statements are genuine expressions of belief and concern. Former Senator Eugene McCarthy observed: "Religious belief, privately held, may well be good for democracy, as John Adams felt. Its politicization is not."[22] An editorial writer has warned about business and political leaders "who proclaim their deep faith in God and ethics but who mostly just believe in money, status, and power."[23] One of the most powerful religious expressions of any president can be found in Abraham Lincoln's second inaugural address, with its several references to God, yet the deeply religious Lincoln is the only president we have had who belonged to no church, though he attended services fairly regularly. When candidates and office-holders invoke religion in their cause, caution is advised. Judging their motivation is difficult—just as judging our own often is.

THE U.S. SUPREME COURT for decades has followed a general rule that "excessive entanglement" between organized religion and our government must be avoided. So, a student can attend Southern Methodist or Notre Dame or Brandeis and receive loans or grants for tuition, just as he or she can if the choice is the University of Oregon or Southern Illinois University. Federal government payments can go to hospitals that have no religious affiliation or are Catholic, Protestant, Jewish, or—perhaps one of these days—Muslim.

Many quote Thomas Jefferson's letter in which he talks about "a wall of separation between church and state." They say they advocate that. But if the local Methodist church is on fire, no one shouts "Separation of church and state! We can't call out the fire department!" I have yet to hear anyone suggest changing the name of St. Louis or St. Paul or Los Angeles.

Where to draw the line has been—and will continue to be—a matter of controversy. *Washington Post* columnist Mary McGrory complained that the Salvation Army had difficulty qualifying for government subsidy of its clearly successful and humanitarian assistance to the homeless at a rate of $20 per family per night (compared to the District government's expenditure of $100). The Salvation Army failed to qualify because it "encouraged its clients to seek spiritual help."[24] Would this be government subsidizing the teaching of religion? Does the government answer make sense? Where do you draw the line?

Such questions have vexed government and civic and religious leaders from the early days of our nation. In his seventh annual message to Congress (now called the State of the Union address), President Ulysses S. Grant recommended a constitutional amendment requiring the states to establish free public schools and "forbidding the teaching in said schools of religious, atheistic or pagan tenets." He also expressed concern about "the accumulation of vast amounts of untaxed church property....I would suggest the taxation of all property equally, whether church or corporation, exempting only the last resting place of the dead and possibly, with proper restrictions, church edifices."[25] Three months earlier he had addressed a group of veterans in Des Moines, Iowa, and said, "Leave the matter of religion to the family circle, the church, and the private school, supported entirely by private contribution. Keep the church and state forever separate."[26] However, Napoleon had a different view, one that many leaders of other nations have followed: "A nation must have a religion, and that religion must be under the control of the government."[27]

We have in our armed forces chaplains who are Catholic, Protestant, Jewish, and Muslim; they receive their pay from the federal government. Many prisons have tax-paid chaplains. There are countless examples of our government and religious authorities working together, cooperating. Where we draw the line ultimately rests with the U.S. Supreme Court and the court of public opinion.

Precisely three years before the terrorist attacks on the World Trade Center, on September 11, 1998, President Bill Clinton had a group of religious leaders to the White House for breakfast and made a public confession of wrongdoing, speaking to the American public through them. This unusual manifestation of our cultural mix of politics and religion was not legally challenged. Neither is the annual Presidential Prayer Breakfast launched by President Eisenhower, an event I usually attended during my years in Washington, though I did so with uneasiness because I had the feeling it was more show than religion.

The uncertain division between faith and government leads to inconsistencies, though I long ago learned that inconsistencies are part of human nature for all of us. The early leading Baptist, Roger Williams, cut the cross out of the king's flag flying over Salem in the Plymouth colony, and some of his Baptist heirs today are in a sense trying to put it back into the flag. While their ancestors strongly advocated separating the spheres of government and religion, many of today's Baptists favor bringing them back together, with prayers in public schools, vouchers for parochial schools, posting of the Ten Commandments, and tax support for many parochial school functions.

We know that often when our government does good things—such as passage of the Civil Rights Act of 1964—religious leadership plays a key role. In the early 1960s our conscience needed to be prodded and faith authorities did that.

Those who have a religious affiliation and are attendees at services are more likely to be community volunteers, and report "talking with 40 percent more people in the course of the day" than those who do not share such characteristics.[28] Their impact on that part of our society with which they are connected is significant.

But we don't want religious authorities to be running the government, nor do we want government enmeshed in setting policies and running religious organizations.

Those who founded our nation were keenly aware of the abuse of religion. For that reason, Thomas Jefferson suggested that members of the clergy should be banned from holding office, but James Madison persuaded him that this would be a mistake, that all citizens should be treated equally. They did not foresee the Protestant/Catholic clashes in Northern Ireland, but they knew of the bloody Christian crusades against the Muslims and Jews, and of the Thirty Years War (1618–1648), largely a clash between Protestants and Catholics, which killed one-fourth of the population of Europe.

The early decades of our history were marked by continuing animosities, even though the national leadership showed great enlightenment. Not having an established church for the national government did not immediately apply to the states, and not until 1833 did the last state abandon that practice. The first constitution of New York State included this article:

> Whereas the ministers of the Gospel are, by their profession, dedicated to the service of God and the care of souls, and ought not to be diverted from the great duties of their functions; therefore no minister of the Gospel, or priest of any denomination whatsoever, shall at any time hereafter, under any pretence or description whatever, be eligible to, or capable of holding, any civil or military office or place within this State.[29]

The first constitution of the state of Massachusetts said: "It is the right as well as the duty of all men in society publicly and at stated seasons to worship the Supreme Being.... Every denomination of Christians...shall be equally under the protection of the law."[30]

Protestants dominated decision-making, sometimes not wisely. Occasionally attempts to ban parochial schools—almost all Catholic—passed, only to be struck down by the Supreme Court. One historian notes: "In Philadelphia a Catholic student was whipped before his class for refusing to read from the King James Bible, while another was punished for bringing his Douay [Catholic version] Bible to school."[31] In the 1880s and 1890s states had a wave of enforcing Sunday as a day of rest, and Seventh Day Adventists paid fines and served time in jail for working on their own farms. Even the U.S. Supreme Court joined the bandwagon, ruling in *Bucher v. Cheshire Railroad Company* in 1888 that Theodore Bucher, who had sued the railroad for an injury, was not eligible for damages because he had traveled on Sunday, contrary to Massachusetts law.[32] Congress had originally ordered that there be postal deliveries seven days a week, but religious groups quickly pressured the legislators to change that practice.

While occasionally religion has been used to foment hatred in our nation, and we continue to have oddities like those who believe they must show their faith by handling poisonous snakes, there has been a growth in understanding and tolerance—at least until September 11th. We generally understand that belonging to a church or synagogue or mosque does not automatically make a person better or worse than someone who is agnostic or an atheist. And the fact that a person belongs to one of the dominant historic religions in the United States, Christianity and Judaism, does not make that person superior to Muslims or Hindus or Buddhists or people of differing beliefs. We are slowly learning that. After September 11th, President George W. Bush immediately reached out to the Muslim leadership in our nation in a sensitive gesture that all faith groups applauded.

We know a few other things that are significant:

– People who are trying to break the drug habit are more likely to be successful if they belong to a church, synagogue, or mosque, or to a similar religiously oriented group.

– People motivated by attempts to live their faith sponsor soup kitchens, build and rebuild homes, volunteer for medical service in areas of great need abroad, and take a host of other actions that everyone welcomes.

– Religion is a restraint for the individual believer against conduct that can be harmful to society. Even in prisons, wardens sometimes relate that someone is "a changed person" since he or she had a religious experience.

– More Americans observe their religious affiliation by attendance at services on Sunday, Saturday, or Friday than do people in almost any nation. Polls vary a few points, but roughly 40 percent of the American public say they attend religious services at least once a week (apparently a higher claim than the reality), and approximately 55 percent say that religion is a strong influence in their lives. A small indication of trends is that in the year 2000, 61 percent of adult Americans contributed to churches or religious organizations compared to 66 percent the year before, and the average total of donations given by them dropped from $806 to $649.[33] By comparison, fewer than one in ten in France attend a church service once a year and fewer than two percent attend services of the official Church of England regularly.[34] The Philippines, Ireland, Poland, and a few Latin American countries with a heavy Roman Catholic tilt have a higher church attendance rate than we do. But that is atypical. More typical of Europeans is a woman who took religion in school, as most Europeans are required to do, but "no one took it seriously," and not simply at school. "The message I got at home was that it wasn't important."[35]

– If the polls are correct, younger Americans are as religious as their parents in terms of a belief in a deity, but they are less accepting of the dogma of any one group and are less faithful in their religious observances, such as church attendance. They are part of what philosopher Hannah Arendt calls "a crisis of institutional religion."[36]

Robert Putnam writes, "Over the last three to four decades Americans have become about 10 percent less likely to claim church membership, while our actual attendance and involvement in religious activities has fallen by roughly 25 to 50 percent."[37] Largely because of the increasing Hispanic population, Roman Catholic membership continues to grow, as does membership in some of the non-mainline Protestant churches. Mainline Protestant denominations and some Jewish groups are showing a decline. Muslim faith branches have grown, primarily through immigration.

The Institute for American Values says: "What ails our democracy is not simply the loss of certain organizational forms, but the loss of certain organizing ideals—moral ideals that authorize our civic creed."[38]

However, the great abuse of religion in twenty-first-century America is its non-application, with commands of all faiths to help the poor, for example, being observed with pious words but far too few deeds. As one religion observer notes, when there is "virtue" without identification with the larger community, "righteousness becomes self-righteousness."[39] Speaking at the funeral of the four girls killed in the Birmingham church bombing, Martin Luther King Jr. said that their lives and deaths "speak out to every minister of the gospel who has remained silent behind the safe security of stained-glass windows."[40] In speeches to religious leaders he often said, "We suffer from high blood pressure of creeds and an anemia of deeds." A report of a lengthy study of religious beliefs and practices in the British publication, *The Economist*, concludes: "The most successful churches are also the ones that require a lot of their members."[41] Former UN secretary general Dag Hammerskjöld, not a theologian but a reflective person, wrote: "In our own era, the road to holiness necessarily passes through the world of action."[42]

MOST PEOPLE WOULD RECOGNIZE religion as a force for good in our nation, even though extremists abuse it. But there are areas of inconsistency, of dilemma.

Why is this religiously oriented nation among the worst in the world in terms of crimes of violence? Why do we have the highest rate of incarceration of prisoners of any nation? Why do we have more African American males in prisons and jails than in universities?

When all faiths require aid to the poor, why do we have a higher percentage of our children living in poverty than any other industrial nation? Why is the United States—which once led in response to world poverty under the Marshall Plan—now last among the world's twenty-two wealthy nations in the percentage of our income that goes for helping the poor beyond our borders?

THERE ARE NO SIMPLE ANSWERS. But three conclusions can be drawn:

First, while we respect the right of people to be atheists or anarchists or follow any dogma, religion has been generally a force for good in our nation, but it is wise to maintain a healthy but not rigid separation between church and state.

Second, each of us lives our faith inconsistently, and what is true of our individual lives is true of the collective religious and political entities to which we belong.

Third, freedom of religion is a huge asset to our nation, one we must cherish.

CHAPTER THREE

THE WORLD FAMILY

Children who go unheeded are children who are going to turn on the world that neglected them.

—Robert Coles, Psychiatrist[1]

Each year my children and grandchildren come together with us for a week of vacation, so that we can get to know each other better and establish a sense of greater kinship. That kinship is legally already established, but—too often in an age when families scatter more and more—the technical legal ties of family are weaker than they should be because we don't talk to one another, we don't listen to one another.

We occasionally hear the phrase "the human family," suggesting that all of us have a kinship, implying that we should work together and get to understand each other better. That sounds so obvious it is almost trite to repeat. But a family that lives under one roof ultimately cannot be healthy in physical goods or mental attitude if it does not recognize its involvement in the larger family. St. Paul talks about "the whole family in heaven and earth."[2]

There is a Moroccan proverb, "None but a mule denies his family."[3] If that is accurate, the world is heavily populated with mules, human mules. Our interdependence is not as widely recognized as it should be.

The members of the core nuclear family we usually have in mind when we use the world "family" have to work at listening to each other, accommodating one another, sharing each other's triumphs and tragedies. The same is true of the larger human family, of the community of nations.

If a member of a small family living in one household announced periodically, "I'm better than the rest of the members of my family," that person might be respected for his money or his muscle, but the family would be headed toward disintegration. Similarly, one nation that is a member of the family of nations cannot either announce or imply or convey an I'm-better-than-you-are attitude—no matter how much muscle and money it has—without causing unfavorable consequences for itself and some disintegration of family unity.

We are part of the large family of humanity and should conduct ourselves in a way that shows that. At the same time, we want to nurture our smaller family that lives under one roof. In both families we must recognize that, while disputes and disagreements will arise, restraint must be exercised. There is occasionally truth to the observation of the late George Burns: "Happiness is having a large, loving, caring, close-knit family in another city."[4]

RESPECT FOR THE IMPORTANCE of a healthy life for that small family is still part of American culture, a basic value, but that value has been marred in our history and too often is sullied today, distorted by our failure to understand that all humanity is part of our family.

In addition to idealistic reasons for having a cohesive family life, a study by an interdisciplinary group of family scholars noted:

> Marriage appears to reduce the risk that children and adults will be either perpetrators or victims of crime. Single and divorced women are four to five times more likely to be victims of violent crime in any given year than married women. Boys raised in single-parent homes are twice as likely (and boys raised in stepfamilies three times as likely)

to have committed a crime that leads to incarceration by the time they reach their early thirties, even after controlling for factors such as race, mother's education, neighborhood quality and cognitive ability.[5]

Single parents—usually women—would not have as great a struggle if we recognized more fully that humanity is not divisible, that we are all family.

If we understood that, it would change individual conduct as well as our collective behavior through government.

One of the almost hidden developments in our society is that we are more economically segregated than at any other time in our nation's history. A study released in May 2003 suggests a slight shift away from that segregated housing pattern. However, wherever you live, the odds are overwhelming that your neighbors are roughly in the same income category. We isolate the poor and in the process do harm to them and to our society. Many public housing projects are segregated not only by race (not technically but in reality) but often legally by income. As soon as a person achieves enough income, he or she is forced to leave the public housing. The result: poor people who are overwhelmed by their problems live next to poor people who are overwhelmed by their problems, and not surprisingly the problems multiply. A high percentage of those who live in public housing projects are single women with children.

Particularly in high-rise public housing, those mothers are afraid to let their children romp in the street or in the play-lot at the development because of high crime. So television becomes the easy way out—television that depicts and glorifies much too much violence. Surveys show that in neighborhoods where there are severe economic problems, children watch approximately twice as much television as their counterparts in middle- and upper-class areas. The quality of the shows they watch is not good for them and, it should be added, too often not good for the image of the United States abroad. William Burrows, managing editor of Orbis Books, notes: "Cultural 'pollution' touches far more people [around the world], far more directly than any other American artifact or business."[6]

Poverty is higher among single mothers, and too many of those mothers have been denied the opportunity for learning basic literacy skills, thus intensifying their poverty and making it less likely that their children will do well in school and emerge from the ranks of the poor. Citizens who volunteer to develop the literacy skills of those in need perform a great public service. One of the effective ways of doing this is for an organization—a church or business or civic group—to take this on as a special project. Even if it is done for only one year, it is of help to both the trainer and the trainee. The person who becomes a teacher or mentor gains important insights into a sometimes ignored part of our society. I recall visiting an IBM office in downtown Chicago where volunteers helped people who came to their office from a nearby public housing project, Cabrini Green. It meant office managers taking some risk, tutors giving some time, and women from the housing project exercising some courage by walking into a totally strange environment. I have no gauge of the results, but I know that everyone benefited. In a good way, all of them became family.

Many single parents are not poor. Some are women who have made a choice to give birth to a child despite being single. More and more single people who have chosen not to marry have voluntarily adopted a child who needs love and attention. This is a change in child-rearing practices, bringing with it an altering of public attitudes. Shunning the single mother is not acceptable in public mores today.

READ THE CORRESPONDENCE between John Adams and Abigail Adams written early in our nation's history and you will learn about two stimulating adults with a healthy but not totally untroubled family life—except for long periods of absence in which duties for the fledgling American government required the father in that family to be away from home.

What were the barriers to a healthy family life then? Some

were the same as ours, caused by "the weakness of human flesh." But many were different.

- Women then generally played a visibly secondary role. There were few, if any, wedding ceremonies that did not require the bride to *obey* her husband-to-be. Women could not vote and, in most jurisdictions, could not testify in court or be on a jury. They also had limited ability to own property.

- Abuse of women was more commonly accepted early in our history, as it is today in most developing nations. "They have to learn to respect you," many men said. To gain that respect, occasionally—sometimes frequently— men resorted to physical violence.

- Families were large and deaths in childhood or for mothers in childbirth were frequent. At the turn of the century, water-borne diseases—malaria, cholera, and diarrhea—were the principal killers of children after the age of one, just as they continue to be in the developing world today.

- The average marriage did not last as long as it does in the twenty-first century, despite the fact that divorces were much less frequent. The reason: earlier deaths. In the year 2002, the average American lives to be seventy-seven; a century ago it was forty-eight. During my youth, if a couple celebrated a fiftieth wedding anniversary it was considered a major event because of its rarity. Today even sixtieth wedding anniversaries are not that uncommon.

- African Americans who were slaves did not have birth dates recorded. Ordinarily they had only one name, for example Sarah or Bill, and formal marriages were rare so that any male or female could be sold at the owner's convenience. Residues of that forced family separation remain today.

Before her death, anthropologist Margaret Mead observed that never before has a nuclear family lived "all by itself in a box" with no relatives and other social support systems."[7] She might have added that we now live in a special kind of box, mesmerized by a box, television, that has diminished family dialogue. The idyllic summer scene of family members in front of their home, two of them on a wooden swing on the porch visiting with their neighbors, is almost history. Air conditioning has shoved us into the box we call our home, and we visit less with those who live near us.

Changes in recent decades—other than increased single parenthood—are viewed as either good or bad, depending on your perspective. These changes include the following:

- Families are much smaller. Farm families often had ten to twelve children, as did immigrant families and others in the miserably poor urban areas. In time of economic hardship, with nothing like unemployment compensation and other social safety nets to which we're accustomed, many urban dwellers gave up children to relatives or friends or orphanages, a heart-breaking necessity. With today's smaller families and the social protections that have evolved, traditional orphanages in the United States are extinct, and families will rarely feel compelled by economic necessity to turn their children over to others. There are social advantages to the larger family, and some yearn for "the good old days," which will never return.

- People are marrying later in life. Teenage marriages are rarer. More married couples are opting not to have children. Divorce is less common for those not marrying "too young."

– Women have a much greater opportunity to work, and not simply as teachers, nurses, clerical aids, or kitchen assistants and housekeepers for those more economically advantaged. This greater opportunity means a higher standard of living for families, more home ownership, a greater chance for a family vacation, and other benefits. However, the loss of time the mother has with children is widely, though not universally, regarded as on the debit side of the ledger. Women should be free to make the choice, but present-day attitudes sometimes create uncomfortable situations. A few decades ago, when I met a couple I would inquire of the man what he did and then often the wife would mention her occupation if she had a job. Now I will ask both husband and wife what they do, and frequently the woman will say, with some embarrassment, "I'm only a housewife and mother." I feel an awkwardness for having asked the question, but I also tell that person, "You have a most important job!" I hope we can soon reach the point at which women and men can feel comfortable saying they are attorneys or engineers or full-time parents. Our culture has changed to the point that in some households men now stay home and take care of the children full time, and that number will grow.

Former vice president Al Gore and his wife Tipper noted in a book on family life: "The *quality* of family life is suffering because so many working parents are now chronically exhausted, stretched thin, and stressed out. In the last twenty years, the sharp increase in the number of hours worked outside the home by mothers as well as fathers—along with the dramatic increase in the number of single parents—has placed new strains on families."[8]

Another thing that has changed is our divorce rate. It is now much higher and the social stigma once coupled with divorce has diminished appreciably.

One healthy change that has accompanied the cultural shift to expanding the roles for women is that in many areas, more women, particularly single mothers, are involved in civic activity.

There is a feeling on the part of the more conservative community that women should stay home and take care of their children when they are young—although poor women should be working. Columnist Ellen Goodman writes:

> Anyone who listened to the [debate] surrounding the welfare reauthorization bill knows that poor and single mothers are not described as "stay-at-home moms." They are not lauded as women doing "the hardest job in the world." Welfare mothers are, rather, women who need to discover the "dignity and self-worth" that comes from real jobs. Their children don't need them at home; they need them in the workplace as "role models."[9]

She writes in the same column: "I worked outside my home throughout motherhood. I think the balance of work and family is as rewarding as it is stressful."

Also getting mixed reviews is an openness about social behavior that a few years ago in most instances would have evoked family and public censure. Couples may live together prior to marriage, colleges have coed dorms, and gay couples are often open about their relationships. How much of this is changed conduct is not clear. Some is. Regardless of what a person's attitude toward gays may be, isolation from family and friends is less frequent and that is good. Going through the period of sexual maturation is difficult enough for young people who follow the conventional patterns, and those whose sexual orientation differs from most of us face even greater emotional problems. Their suicide rate is high. Like all young people, they should feel surrounded by family and friends who genuinely care about them. The scientific evidence that homosexuality involves a genetic disposition among males is now widely accepted, and the presumption is that when similar studies are completed on lesbian orientation the results will be the same.

A friend from college days told me about his daughter telling him that she is a lesbian. "Why did you choose that lifestyle?" he asked her. "Dad," she responded incredulously, "you don't believe I *chose* this lifestyle, do you?"

Negative influences on children and young people can be the many things that disrupt family cohesion as well as the powerful "sermons" delivered by the medium of television, sermons portraying dysfunctional family life, violence, crude language, and the not-so-subtle message that if you simply had more material things life would be so much better. The advertising appeals for everything from children's games to new cars, from soap to cosmetics, from fancy clothes to expensive toys feed a false sense of values to those who are mesmerized by TV. Those same advertising appeals and the content of much of our entertainment programming reach the family of humanity beyond our borders with a message that Americans are totally absorbed in acquiring mountains of material goods and have little concern about the impoverished within or beyond our borders. Glorified selfishness is portrayed as the idol we worship, and unfortunately there is an element of truth to that.

There are constructive children's programs on public television and, as children get older, they can watch worthwhile presentations on CSPAN, the History and Discovery channels, and a few others. Making time to watch television with them, explain things, and stress constructive activity rather than simply using TV as a baby-sitting device is important. But it is rare. There are wholesome TV shows, yet on balance television has to be viewed as a negative for family and community life unless careful limitations are put on its use for children and self-discipline is exercised by adults. Television is distorting our priorities.

When asked by Roper pollsters in 1975 to identify the elements of "the good life," 38 percent of all American adults chose "a lot of money," and another 38 percent mentioned "a job that contributes to the welfare of society." By 1996 those who aspired to contribute to society had slipped to 32 percent, while those who aspired to a lot of money had leaped to 63 percent.[10]

TV is not solely responsible for these distorted values, but it is a cause.

For whatever reason, families are visiting other families less than they formerly did, and having friends to your home for dinner is a declining activity, according to Robert Putnam's book, *Bowling Alone*.[11]

"FAMILY" IS MORE THAN a nuclear entity living in a nice white house isolated from its neighbors and the rest of the world. Those who understand the ripple effects of everything we do know that family includes our community, our nation, and our world. Somehow we are connected with people in Africa suffering from hunger, with victims of a confusing civil war in the Congo. To deny that connection, not overtly but through indifference, is to deny to those immediately around us the knowledge that concern for others is essential for the well-being of all of us.

When I am speaking to groups, someone in the audience will often ask, "Shouldn't we pay more attention to our problems at home and not spend so much money on foreign aid?" I respond that we should, of course, pay more attention to our difficulties at home, but I have observed in my years in politics that those who support with more than lip service doing something about our troubles at home are the same people who vote and care and act on behalf of those who face difficulties beyond our borders. And then I ask the person to guess how much of the federal budget goes for foreign economic assistance. Almost always the answer is 15 to 25 percent. When I explain that it is now less than one-half of one percent of the budget, the person is usually surprised.

I give a few more statistics and then I tell them about a visit I made to Malawi, in southern Africa, while neighboring Mozambique was in the throes of a civil war. At that time, the average income per year in Malawi was just over $100 and the nation's population was less than eight million. The country had approximately one million refugees from Mozambique. That would be comparable to the United State having thirty-five million refugees. (Many in our nation seemed terrified when one year we had two hundred thousand refugees from Cuba.)

I visited a refugee camp in the southern part of Malawi, the biggest one I had ever seen with forty thousand refugees. The camp director asked if I would be willing to talk to some of the people, and he arranged them in three groups: men, women, and children. They sat on the ground. We had no public address system. I shouted and the interpreter shouted after me. When I spoke to the children, I noticed a small boy sitting about twenty feet in front of me. Perhaps ten years old, he had a badly infected eye over which insects were crawling.

After our brief program, I asked the camp director if something could be done to help that boy. "We can only take care of emergencies," he replied. I have never forgotten that small child. I don't know how his future ties in with the future of my four grandchildren, but instinctively I know it does—and you know it does. I tell my students over and over again: Humanity is not divisible. We are one family.

Jesus told the story about a man now known as the "Good Samaritan." That is not a biblical phrase. A more accurate description would be "the hated Samaritan." Jesus told of a man stopped and beaten by robbers on the winding road from Jerusalem to Jericho, a dangerous road then and no less dangerous today, but for different reasons. The man needed help. Walking by on the other side of the road to avoid him were a member of the clergy and someone from the tribe of Levi, a privileged class. The person who stopped was a Samaritan, someone looked down upon by the people to whom Jesus spoke.

The story came in response to an audience question, "Who is my neighbor?" Jesus' answer made the audience uncomfortable. I am sure it would be the same if Jesus were speaking to us. The persons passing by today might be an active religionist, perhaps a wealthy (by the rest of the world's standards) American. The person who stopped? You name the most unpopular person in your area. Perhaps the town drunk; perhaps a Communist; perhaps the community's outspoken atheist or anarchist.

We need to squirm and to feel uncomfortable. See the pictures and read the stories of those who suffer from AIDS in Africa. What are we doing to help? Is ignoring them good for our immediate family? How do we define family?

FAMILY INCLUDES THE ELDERLY. Because of our high rate of geographical dispersal after high school, college, and marriage, children are less likely to have meaningful relationships with their grandparents, a loss to both generations.

Grandparents tend to be good listeners. Outside my window as I type this is a large deer, eating grass from the remnants of last fall's lawn. Periodically deer stop what they're doing, pull their heads up high, and listen. They have sensitive hearing. As a grandfather I speak with some prejudice, but I have observed in other grandparents the quality that deer have: sensitive hearing. Perhaps those elders wear hearing aids, but they are interested and concerned with what their grandchildren have to say. If grandparents are not in your vicinity, finding an older couple or person living alone to help with "sitting" or visiting gives children a chance to communicate and enrich older people, and provides a stimulus to both old and young.

Older citizens normally face greater health problems than their younger relatives and friends do. How does our society help them? We have Medicare for seniors, but often the bills at the pharmacy make handling other necessities almost impossible. What can we do as a society? What are you doing as a relative or friend of an older person to assist with special needs? Eventually many older people will have to be placed in assisted living units or nursing homes. Can they handle this financially? Should our society be doing a better job through government to manage these needs?

THE BEST OF VALUES in a family are summed up in a simple word: love. Members should know they are loved, no matter what happens. If there is a drug problem, if someone goes to prison for larceny, if AIDS develops—no matter what happens—members of a family should feel themselves surrounded by love. There are small steps that can make that easier:

- Do things together. Watching television together is rarely *doing* something. Limit the amount of television watched, and when the children are younger look carefully at the quality of the television shows they are watching. Programs with too much entertainment violence, for example, are harmful.

- Plan a family vacation. That's more important than turning in your used car for a new one. The memories of that vacation will last much longer than your memories of a new car. If possible, even after children are grown and geographically scattered, try bringing together children and grandchildren for a week of family vacation. This will help to secure family ties.

- Create opportunities for members of the family to tell each other about new things they have learned, or about a book someone has enjoyed, or about something unusual that happened. Use these sessions to encourage reaching beyond the usual topics of conversation. Mention an article in that day's newspaper about a family that died in a fire in substandard housing, and what you can do about it; about orphans in Romania who have no home; about things that will sensitize everyone present

49

to the realities and the family of the world beyond them. Doing this when your family gets together for a meal is the natural time, though getting together for breakfast, lunch, or dinner has to be mutually planned, particularly as the children get older. Having a family meal together has declined over the last twenty years from 50 percent of American families doing this to 34 percent, according to one survey, but that does not present the full dismal picture, because in *many* households (one survey says *most*) the television set is on during that family meal.[12]

- If possible, make your home not too far from where you work. According to a Department of Transportation survey, the average American adult spends seventy-two minutes a day driving a car. Part of that time may be with children, but seventy-two minutes a day is more time than the average parent spends with his or her children.[13]

Robert Putnam writes:

Virtually all forms of family togetherness became less common over the last quarter of the twentieth century. Between 1976 and 1997, according to Roper polls of families with children eight to seventeen, vacationing together fell from 53 percent to 38 percent, watching TV together from 54 percent to 41 percent, attending religious services together from 38 percent to 31 percent, and "just sitting and talking" together from 53 percent to 43 percent. It is hard not to read these figures as evidence of rapidly loosening family bonds.[14]

When you combine these statistics with the survey of families sharing meals together, Putnam's conclusion is reinforced. Most of us have seen this trend either in our own families or in the families of our relatives and friends.

It is probably true that after a family has scattered greater contact is maintained than in earlier periods because of the changes in technology. A Nebraska friend of mine sends an e-mail every day to each of his family members scattered from Japan to Washington D.C. We can speak on the telephone today with much greater ease and clarity to the remotest spots in the world, thanks to wireless technology and the improvements in land lines. That is good. Lost somewhat is the old-fashioned habit of letter-writing, somehow more personal (this is perhaps my own nostalgia) and more likely to be preserved for reading and rereading.

Whatever mechanism we use for reaching one another after leaving home, it is not a substitute for the needed improvements in the bonding of the family before it scatters.

That bonding becomes more significant for members of the immediate family if they sense it is a coming together not simply for self-satisfaction, but a coming together also to help the large family of humanity.

CHAPTER FOUR

RESTRAINT

Self-discipline is more important than self-indulgence.
—Alan Wolfe, 2001[1]

If you were to ask a representative sampling of observers from other nations to outline the values of the people and government of the United States, few would list restraint. Within our nation, within our communities, and within our families, it is frequently exercised and expected. Yet in our international involvements and statements, restraint is often not evident.

Fifty years after the founding of our nation, perhaps as many as one-fourth of our adult citizens were alcoholics. The excesses in that pre-automobile America did not cause as much carnage as they do today, but they did result in major difficulties. Per capita consumption of alcoholic beverages was approximately ten times as much then.[2]

Smoking of cigarettes has declined significantly. Anyone who travels abroad frequently, as I do, can relate stories of attending meetings in other nations where the majority of participants smoke as the session progresses, and I can remember meetings in our country where a majority smoked. Decisions in "smoke-filled rooms" became part of the American political legend. But no more. There is less restraint in some areas, such as marital faithfulness, than formerly existed, but the overall picture of individual conduct appears to be improved. On a national level, our top leaders have usually shown restraint, at least in domestic political matters, thus contributing to the stability of the nation.

When Richard Nixon lost a close race to John F. Kennedy, he could have called for demonstrations on the street to protest the result. A few advisers urged him to contest the election. Instead, whether he felt like doing it or not, he knew the right thing to do would be to congratulate the winner, and he did it. The mantle of leadership in the world's most powerful nation passed peacefully to John F. Kennedy without a shot being fired, without even fifty people gathering anywhere to protest. A few years later, Richard Nixon defeated Hubert Humphrey in another close race, and the Democratic candidate congratulated Nixon. In another small gesture appreciated by many of us, Richard Nixon, emerging from the isolation into which he had retreated after his disgrace, made his first public appearance at the Washington, D.C., memorial service for Humphrey, following the Minnesotan's death.

When Albert Gore Jr. received more popular votes than George W. Bush in the election of 2000, and a messy situation in Florida became the key to winning or losing, the U.S. Supreme Court voted 5-4 to declare George W. Bush the winner, in what many regard as one of the more blatantly political decisions in the history of that court. Vice President Gore could have protested and caused a national furor, but in the best speech of his entire career he said, "I disagree with the Court's decision, but I will abide by it."

If we are driving a car, we do not see how close to the edge of a cliff we can come without falling over. In a stable democracy, we do not see how far we can carry our freedom. We generally understand that self-restraint is needed for a democracy to function effectively.

This understanding has been part of our history from the earliest days.

George Washington, Thomas Jefferson, John Adams, and the other early leaders who headed the fight for our independence from Great Britain urged citizens in the newly independent United States to respect and exercise restraint with those who had been British sympathizers. Benjamin Franklin and John Jay were particularly helpful. But pockets of people calling for revenge could have been aroused had there been different leaders. One prominent Massachusetts clergyman preached a widely distributed sermon based on a text from the book of Joshua: "There is an accursed thing in the midst of thee, O Israel; thou canst not stand before thine enemies, until ye take away the accursed thing from among you" (Joshua 7:13). He made clear that this meant "a serious, deliberate, religious act of justice, which God requires of us."[3] For him, justice meant revenge. But the national leaders did not succumb to that temptation and this resulted in a relatively peaceful but difficult transition toward a national government.

The French Revolution, in contrast, did not have leaders who urged restraint, and while it toppled the monarchy—later to be replaced by Napoleon—the bitterness and the revenge resulted in a badly divided France and what most historians view as a failed revolution. At one point, three hundred thousand suspects were imprisoned and eventually seventeen thousand were executed. The harvest? Deep bitterness. People of strong ideological bent headed the French Revolution. Historian Daniel Boorstin correctly notes: "We are accustomed to think of the American Revolution as the great age of American political thought. It may therefore be something of a shock to realize that it did not produce a single important treatise on political theory."[4] Washington, Jefferson, Hamilton, Adams, Madison, and the others who created what became a nation were practical men. The *Federalist Papers*, which sometimes touched on political philosophy, were letters published to persuade the public and leaders in the individual states, formerly colonies, to support the newly created constitution. Our revolution lacked the excessive passion of the French Revolution and partly because of that resulted in a greater success.

Most histories of our nation go directly from the war to the creation of the government, not even dealing with the question of the treatment of those citizens of the colonies who supported the British. Revenge was not part of our national agenda, as it was in France.

The National Assembly of France approved the Declaration of the Rights of Man on August 26, 1789. Less than a month later, the U.S. Congress approved our Bill of Rights. Both are eloquent documents about fundamental political rights. However, for a substantial period the French document went unheeded by France's rulers, while the U.S. Bill of Rights has continuously provided basic protections. Why the difference? A major distinction was the restraint used by the early U.S. leaders, much greater restraint than that practiced by their French counterparts. Washington and Jefferson and those who piloted our ship of state did not let citizens, in the passion of the moment, trample on the basic liberties of our people. Thomas Paine, whose writings aided our revolution, traveled to France and became a powerful voice for the French Revolution, but when the war ended he favored exile for King Louis XVI, rather than execution, and for this indiscretion the new government imprisoned him for eleven months. That was a minor injustice compared to many actions of the new government of France. The American Revolution did not have what one historian calls "the ominous excesses" of the French Revolution and that show of restraint helped to heal and unify the American colonies into a slowly emerging nation.[5]

Thomas Jefferson was in France for our country when those who drafted our Constitution met. Upon his return, he commented that if he could add one thing to that document it would be to require budgetary restraint. For most of the history of our nation budgetary restraint has been exercised by all presidents and congresses, but in recent years that restraint has diminished. Since 1980 we have far more than doubled the national debt, piling up bills for our children and future generations and increasing the hidden tax of higher interest rates that go with excessive demand from all sources for money. Our early leaders would be stunned to read that we both increase debt and lower taxes at the same time, living it up at the expense of our children. As of this writing, for fiscal year 2004 we will have a record-breaking deficit of almost $400 billion—and also a sizable tax cut. This may be good politics, but it is bad economics. Equally dismaying, a decreasing percentage of our tax dollar goes to help the impoverished in our nation and in other countries (discussed in more detail in chapter 10). Harvard's William Julius Wilson, a thoughtful observer of the national scene, has commented: "People who see some prospect for advancement postpone gratification."[6] We are not postponing gratification as much as we should if we want to advance the future of our children and their children.

When General Ulysses S. Grant accepted General Robert E. Lee's surrender at Appomattox, we might have expected words of exhilaration from Grant after finally winning that bitter Civil War. However, Grant wrote in his journal: "I felt...sad and depressed at the downfall of a foe who had fought so long and valiantly, and had suffered so much for a cause, though that cause...was one of the worst for which a people ever fought."[7] In a nation that then needed restraint, Grant exercised it.

Following World War II, the guns fell silent after 405,000 of our sons and a few of our daughters had been killed by the Germans, Italians, and Japanese. President Harry Truman and General George Marshall, with the cooperation of the Senate Republican leader on foreign policy, Senator Arthur Vandenberg of Michigan, asked the nation to help rebuild Germany, Italy, and Japan. It was this successful and generous—though unpopular—display of restraint, rather than revenge, that has given our generation and those who will live after us a greater chance for a world of peace.

Future historians are likely to look more kindly on the service of President Richard Nixon than are current scribes, but the huge deficit in his record started when he failed to exhibit restraint in his eagerness to make sure that he would defeat the Democrats in the election of 1972. His lack of self-restraint in approving the break-in at the Democratic headquarters at Watergate kept compounding itself with coverup actions, some legal and some illegal.

Examples of success through restraint can also be found in the international arena.

For many years, South Africa had an oppressive system of racial separation known as apartheid. This system was denounced by Roman Catholic, Jewish, and Protestant leaders—including the Dutch Reformed and Anglican officials, who were significant because of the Dutch and British heritage of South Africa. That nation had the good fortune to have as the opposition leader the soon-to-be president of the nation, Nelson Mandela, who urged restraint.

After becoming president, Mandela set up a Truth and Reconciliation Commission, headed by Anglican Archbishop Desmond Tutu. That commission asked people to tell the truth about crimes and then urged the nation to forgive those who had committed them. These people were not prosecuted. The process did not eliminate bitterness, but it did reduce it. None of this would have been possible if Prime Minister F. W. De Clerk had not shown great courage in releasing Nelson Mandela from prison and in calling for voting rights for all South Africans. Nelson Mandela made clear, after emerging from prison, that whites and blacks and coloreds—the three categories in that country—should work together and be treated equally.

In my first visits to South Africa, before Mandela's release, I thought the country would not be able to avoid a bitter, bloody civil war, probably costing millions of lives. But restraint on the part of two remarkable leaders, De Clerk and Mandela—who do not get along well personally—resulted in an infinitely improved situation. I had the good fortune to be at Nelson Mandela's presidential inauguration as part of the official U.S. delegation. Nelson Mandela had invited three of the prison guards who had monitored his incarceration to sit in the VIP section. This was a small gesture that said much about President Mandela and helped in the healing process of South Africa. While Nelson Mandela has strong likes and dislikes, in my limited contacts with him on both public and private occasions, I have never heard him utter a word of bitterness about his twenty-six years of incarceration. There is a Lincolnesque quality of restraint about him that has greatly benefited South Africa.

As I TYPE (yes, on a manual typewriter!) this manuscript, the United States has launched a military invasion of Iraq. I hope the eventual scenario plays out better than I fear. The attack means military personnel losses on our side and the death of many innocent Iraqi civilians; it has the potential to do harm to neighboring Turkey and further destabilize that entire region. This is a judgment call, and my judgment is that the armed intervention was a grave mistake. The old saying is true: Violence begets violence.

After September 11th, world public opinion sympathized with our country. Eighteen months later, a majority of Americans supported the invasion of Iraq, but public opinion polls around the world showed results that are likely to haunt us in the future. Suddenly an overwhelming majority of leaders and people around the world viewed the United States as a greater threat to peace than Iraq. Senator Robert Byrd of West Virginia noted that our aim was to isolate Saddam Hussein, and we have handled things in such a manner that we at least temporarily have isolated the United States.

International law says that if we are in danger of imminent attack, we have the right to a preemptive strike. No one I know believes we were in danger of imminent attack. If the United States can launch such an attack, how are we to speak forcefully if China attacks Taiwan or Mongolia, or if any other nation launches a preemptive strike against another? If we use as an excuse that we are concerned by Iraq's use of chemical and biological weapons (many of the chemicals supplied by us during Iraq's war with Iran) or its nuclear potential, what about Syria, Sudan, Libya, North Korea and other nations with that potential? Are we to invade them all? Or is it wiser to use the type of restraint we exercised against a much greater threat, the Soviet Union? We let the Soviets know forcefully that any use of these weapons against other nations would result in massive retaliation. It worked. Restraint on our part caused restraint by them.

Almost forgotten in the anti-Iraq furor is that our aim is to stop terrorism. An unpopular attack on Iraq in the name of fighting terrorism has already caused further terrorist attacks, and the end of these is not in sight. Once Congress made the mistake of authorizing the President to launch an attack, and it began, I supported our effort, hoping to get the war over quickly. But there will be more attacks on innocents, especially among the more than one million Americans who live outside our country and several times that many who travel each year beyond our borders.

Time magazine recently carried this account:

> On November 3 in a remote area of Yemen, a CIA Predator loosed a Hellfire missile that vaporized a car in which a top al-Qaeda leader, Qaed Salim Sinan al-Harethi, was thought to be riding along with five other people, including an American citizen. The American, believed to be Kamal Derwish, was later described by Administration officials as the leader of an alleged al-Qaeda sleeper cell in New York State. The officials said he persuaded young men from Lackawana, New York, a Buffalo suburb, to travel to Afghanistan for religious studies at locations that turned out to be terrorist training camps. Six members of the group were arrested [in] September and charged with providing material support to a foreign terrorist group.
>
> Perhaps Derwish deserved the fate of the company he kept, or perhaps he was a certified bad guy. Nevertheless, an American citizen not charged or convicted of any crime was killed by a CIA Predator...and there was hardly a peep of protest in the country.[8]

A few weeks later, on December 30, 2002, three American medical missionaries in a remote part of that country were slain.

Both the Yemen and U.S. governments said they had no idea of the motivation of the killers.

If they don't know, I think I do. We killed an apparent terrorist and his companions and indirectly killed three Baptist missionaries. That type of story is likely to be repeated many times unless we handle ourselves with great adeptness now that the Iraq conflict has ended.

I am not in love with Saddam Hussein any more than I admired Stalin or Brezhnev, the Soviet leaders. I visited Iraq one time. The afternoon that I arrived, the diplomatic community in Baghdad was aroused. An Iraqi employee of the British embassy had provided that post with statistics about agricultural production in Iraq, statistics that the employee thought of as having no military significance. Saddam, however, viewed the action as espionage. The man was arrested that afternoon and executed within an hour. The question is not whether Saddam Hussein and other dictators are brutal. The question is how we limit them. Effectiveness will require restraint on our part, not an emotional response.

Some of us are old enough to remember when many responsible leaders were saying that a war with the Soviet Union was inevitable, and that we should attack them first. The Soviets posed a much greater threat than Iraq. In 1950, Secretary of the Navy Francis Matthews said that the United States must be ready "to pay any price, even the price of instituting a war to compel cooperation for peace."[9] In response, President Harry Truman said: "There is nothing more foolish than to think that war can be stopped by war. You don't prevent anything but peace."[10]

When a baseball strike seemed imminent in the United States, one sportswriter wrote that two things, once started, can easily go out of control: strikes and war.

He is correct.

BEFORE THE ATTACK on Iraq, an unusual number of faith leaders of all persuasions urged restraint by the U.S. That is a new phenomenon. There always have been a few in every potential conflict urging restraint, but I am encouraged by the increased sensitivity of religious leaders on this life/death issue of war with its growing number of civilian deaths.

For centuries and in all nations religious leaders have tended to sanctify the cause of their country's wars and pray for victory over the evil foes. When Filipino revolutionaries who had fought Cuban occupation continued to fight after the Philippine Islands were transferred to the United States, our government tried semi-successfully to suppress that uprising in 1899 to 1902. Faith leaders in our country joined with prayers and speeches in support of that effort. Mark Twain submitted a "prayer" to *Harper's Bazaar* that the magazine did not publish:

> O Lord our God, help us to tear their soldiers to bloody shreds with our shells; help us to cover their smiling fields with the pale forms of their patriot dead; help us to drown the thunder of the guns with the shrieks of their wounded, writhing in pain; help us to lay waste their humble homes with a hurricane of fire; help us to wring the hearts of their unoffending widows with unavailing grief; help us to turn them out roofless with their little children to wander un-friended in the wastes of their desolated land in rags and hunger and thirst.[11]

No AMERICAN LEADER is more widely revered in this nation and in others than Abraham Lincoln. There is also no better example than his of leadership that shows restraint. He is revered for freeing the slaves, and his assassination adds a dramatic touch. It is worth noting that Presidents William McKinley and James Garfield were also assassinated and they have nowhere near Lincoln's stature. The "something more" quality that Lincoln had was a greatness of spirit.

In his second inaugural address, when it appeared that the Union cause finally was prevailing after a bitter, bitter struggle, the leader of this fractured nation might have been expected to say, "We're going to beat those doers of dastardly deeds." After all, only ten months earlier in the Battle of the Wilderness of Spotsylvania and Cold Harbor, Virginia, Northern troops under the command of General Ulysses Grant suffered almost sixty thousand casualties, more than twenty-four thousand deaths. In a nation of 31 million people, 623,000 men lost their lives in the Civil War. This was one out of every eleven men in the military age group. To better understand that war's bitterness, that loss—623,000 out of 31 million—we can compare it to 117,000 U.S. personnel killed in World War I in a nation of 103 million; 405,000 in World War II with our 139 million; 54,000 in the Korean War when we had 160 million; and 58,000 in the Vietnam War in a nation of 218 million. The intense bitterness of the Civil War, both within families and between regions, exceeded anything we had or have known. Many yearned for Lincoln to condemn the Southerners. Instead, the president said:

> With malice toward none; with charity for all; with firmness in the right, as God gives us to see the right, let us strive on to finish the work we are in; to bind up the nation's wounds; to care for him who shall have borne the battle, and for his widow, and his orphan—to do all which may achieve and cherish a just, and a lasting peace, among ourselves, and with all nations.

There were those in the North who wanted to try as many as one million Southerners for treason. Lincoln, in a sense, pardoned the South in this inaugural address. After the bloodiest of our wars, only one person had to face trial—and not for treason, but for murder. The superintendent of the Andersonville Prison, who had ordered several Union prisoners shot, faced a trial and was hanged.

Unfortunately, after Lincoln's death the victors displayed less restraint than Lincoln espoused and that deficiency added to a bitterness between the North and the South that lasted for decades.

Thanks to Lincoln's speech and actions, violence occurred rarely. Still, because of the speech and actions of others, the spirit of revenge and hatred penetrated the political and economic arenas.

Those in positions of authority, and the citizens who serve with and under them, must make it possible for change to take place with as little bitterness as possible, no matter how strongly people feel on issues. Martin Luther King Jr. frequently quoted this line from John F. Kennedy: "Those who make peaceful revolution impossible will make violent revolution inevitable."[12] This nation and this world must more and more become a place where peaceful revolution can take place.

That requires restraint.

CHAPTER FIVE

PARTICIPATION

Snowflakes are one of nature's most fragile things, but just look what they can do when they stick together.

—Verna M. Kelly[1]

When Alexis de Tocqueville visited the United States in 1831, he wrote that we are a nation run more by volunteers than by government. There is much truth to what he said. Tocqueville praised everyone taking "an active part in the government of society."[2] He observed a phenomenon at which visitors to our nation continue to marvel: "Americans form associations for the smallest undertakings."[3]

We are at our best when we are a nation of constructive participants.

Shortly after World War II, my assignment with Army intelligence had me living in a house in a marvelous community in Germany called Coburg, a city of forty thousand best known for having produced the Duke of Coburg, Prince Albert, who married Queen Victoria of England. My stay of slightly more than a year gave me an opportunity to get acquainted with a culture that had survived both a brutal dictatorship and a devastating war that caused casualties in almost every German family. One day as I visited with what we call high school students, it struck me that in our culture we don't vote for the first time when we reach eighteen. We vote for a fourth-grade class president. We vote for the president of the Spanish club. We vote for a homecoming queen. From our early youth on we are participants in one way or another in our democracy.

Or we are not participants!

The percentage of our eligible citizens who vote in elections is universally recognized as an embarrassment. Less than 20 percent of voters turn out for most municipal and school board elections. In 1960, 65.4 percent of the eligible voters went to the polls in the John Kennedy–Richard Nixon race. In 1996, with Bill Clinton, Bob Dole, and Ross Perot in the battle, 50.8 percent voted; in 2000—George W. Bush vs. Al Gore—53.8 percent turned out.[4] Of 172 nations that have some form of elections—not all democracies—the United States is 139th in percentage of voter turnout.[5]

Robert Putnam found declining participation by Americans in many areas. But the deficiency in politics represents a particular threat to our free system. One survey found that political interest had dropped by one-fifth between 1975 and 1999.[6] Particularly discomforting is the lack of interest by young people. Putnam writes: "Daily newspaper readership among people under thirty-five dropped from two-thirds in 1965 to one-third in 1990, at the time that TV news viewership in this same age group fell from 52 percent to 41 percent. Today's under-thirties pay less attention to the news and current events than their elders do or than people their age did two or three decades ago."[7]

Some citizens lament, "The candidates don't stand for anything." Occasionally there is truth to that, and the elevation of scientific polling to find what the public believes has aggravated and escalated that excuse, because spineless candidates gravitate to poll results. However, usually the person who makes such a statement is really professing his or her ignorance and/or lack of interest, because rarely are there two candidates for a major office who do not have a few sharply distinctive planks. Not voting is only one sign of an unhealthy trend toward nonparticipation. Former Wisconsin state legislator and activist Midge Miller comments: "Once you are a parent you can be a good parent or a bad parent, but you can't be a non-parent. Citizenship is the same. You can be a good citizen or a bad citizen, but you can't be a non-citizen."[8]

WE USE THE TERM "war" glibly.

We have a war on cancer, a war on poverty, and now a war on terrorism. Cancer is a threat, poverty is a threat, and terrorism is a threat. Whether it is accurate to describe these as wars, we are in battles with each, and in all of them we have been partially successful. But success in each depends on our willingness to sacrifice.

When North Korea invaded South Korea, President Harry Truman consulted with leaders in Congress and other nations and responded vigorously. He announced a ten-point program to Congress. The last point, simple and straightforward, was to raise taxes. All Americans were asked to sacrifice, and not only with taxes. We had a military draft and economic status did not exempt anyone. We went through that war, almost unbelievably, with no increase in the deficit and the nation's economy in good shape. Many of us who served in the armed forces during that time period benefited in unexpected ways: Harry Truman had integrated the armed forces, and in my Army basic training unit were men who had never come into real social contact with those of other races and religions and regions. This was not a group of Ph.D.s who danced around the crucial racial issues, but men of varying backgrounds who often bluntly and at first insensitively discussed relationships.

Then came the Vietnam War, a real war, though we did not legally call it that. We slipped into it gradually, at first only with small numbers. Then those numbers grew and grew and grew. International support was less solid than it had been during the Korean War. President Lyndon Johnson saw the cost of the war escalating, but he feared Congress would be unwilling to ask the American people for the revenue sacrifice necessary, and since Social Security retirement funds were temporarily running a large surplus, he asked for a change that caused little stir and attention:

merge the Social Security Retirement Fund with the rest of the budget. It hid the cost of the war and called for almost no financial sacrifice by our people. The president hoped that the war would soon end, but he was a president with little background in international affairs. He followed the lead of his military and other advisers and things got worse and worse.

One other striking difference from the Korean War: In the Vietnam era, students were exempt from the draft. That meant, for all practical purposes, that if you had enough money to go to college, you had a good chance of not being sent to Vietnam. The personal sacrifice would generally be made by those whose families could not afford to send them to college. The economic injustice added to a growing feeling of discontent with the war, and soon demonstrations—sometimes violent—were part of the scene in America, as well as in other countries. A president whose record of domestic issues was stellar found himself the subject of intense hatred by many.

Desert Storm was quick and the terrain easy for a well-equipped armed force. Casualties on both sides were minimal compared to most conflicts, and Saudi Arabia, one of the beneficiaries, primarily bore the financial burden.

Now we have "a preemptive strike" against Iraq. It should not be an opening wedge for doing more of that in the future. Wars breed more wars. I am not a pacifist. I served in our armed forces. But the too-easy movement toward military engagement, particularly on the part of those who have never seen the gruesomeness of war, should be restrained. It is easy and popular and usually unwise to talk tough.

The tough talk today is not matched by any call for sacrifice on our part unless you are a member of the armed forces. The estimated cost—$75 billion for the first thirty days—is not matched with any suggestion that any of us who are civilians should sacrifice one tiny iota, even though we are already running a record-breaking deficit that is at least slightly responsible for the depression of the stock market. Instead of asking us to support this effort with a pay-as-you-go small tax increase as Harry Truman did in the Korean War, we are being told that we need to increase defense expenditures by large amounts—and that we should get tax cuts as a bonus. That may be great for me, but not for my grandchildren from whom we will be borrowing the money.

Is there any uniformity of sacrifice except for those serving in the armed forces? I am proud of those who serve, but only their small number are being asked to risk their lives. We can turn on our TVs and view any bombs and gunfire from the safety of our living rooms.

The evil of bloodshed and homeless refugees—one million in the Desert Storm operation—is compounded by the self-deluding process that sanctifies our motives and our actions and vilifies the opposition. Looking through that distorted lens, we march off to kill and maim and slaughter with pride.

The world view of us is to a large extent that of a wild-west cowboy who makes ill-informed decisions on impulse. President Theodore Roosevelt suggested, "Speak softly but carry a big stick." We have the big stick, but we are not speaking softly.

We need citizens who are willing to participate in government—most will not do it as public officials—with the courage to advocate restraint when the macho answers are popular. Simply sitting at home and criticizing the president or members of the House and Senate may be emotionally satisfying, but it does not change policy.

WHAT SHOULD THE PRESIDENT be asking of us?

If your memory is excellent, you may remember that I once sought the Democratic nomination for president. I mention this only because I have focused on that office and its responsibilities and potential more than most people have.

What I know from my years in government and from reading and writing history is that we cannot drift into becoming a greater and better nation; we cannot do it by pandering to every special interest. There is no way we can become a nobler nation by following this unspoken message from too many in both political parties: "We're going to build a better nation, and we're going to do it without any sacrifice on your part. We'll even give you huge tax cuts. We're going to give you an easy, comfortable slide into greatness."

If I want to improve my home, it will require at least a small sacrifice on my part. If we want to improve our country, it will require at least a small sacrifice on our part.

What should we do—and not do? What would be a sensible program for the nation?

On Foreign Policy

- Lift foreign economic assistance from less than one-half of one percent of the budget to two percent of the budget. It would accomplish huge benefits for the poor around the world, ultimately helping us also, and it would dramatically alter our image as "the rich guy who pays no attention to the impoverished."

- Don't break treaties with other nations without their approval.

- Reexamine and approve these international cooperative efforts where we are in opposition: banning of land mines; agreeing with other nations on earth warming; participation in the International Criminal Court; outlawing the sale of small weapons to people in any nation without the approval of that nation's government; and others. We should lead in building a more cooperative world, as we once did, not drag our feet.

- Remember John F. Kennedy's words: "Let us never negotiate out of fear. But let us never fear to negotiate." Talking, communicating on trade issues, and encouraging Americans to travel abroad are practical, needed policies. Economic or diplomatic isolation of another country does not work unless almost all the nations join the effort, as they did in the case of South Africa. Our Cuban policy makes no sense. Talking with leaders there and in Iran, Iraq, Libya, North Korea, and other places can only help.

On Domestic Policy

- Examine areas where there is a long-term payoff— including education, basic research, and medical research —and support them more.

- Make sure all Americans have basic, quality health protection.

- Put government on a pay-as-you-go basis. Where we want increased benefits, we must be willing to tax ourselves. If we are unwilling to tax ourselves, we shouldn't get the services. Not following this policy weakens the economy and increases government's expenditures for interest, a regressive redistribution of wealth.

- Raise college student aid to at least half of what it was under the GI Bill after World War II. In inflation-adjusted dollars, the GI Bill today would average slightly more than a $12,000 grant per academic year. Our present slide downward, compared to rising college costs, is harming the long-range interests of the nation.

- Take whatever steps are possible within recent court decisions to encourage diversity on college campuses, so that students learn an immensely important non-credit lesson: We all have the same hopes and fears and must work together.

– Inaugurate a program to greatly expand our now minuscule efforts to have U.S. college students study abroad.

– Increase assistance to pre-school, elementary, and high school programs, with special aid to those who enrich their curriculum with foreign language study and to those who sponsor a longer school year.

– Initiate a WPA-type program where people who cannot find a job can work for the government as an employer of last resort, at the minimum wage, four days a week; it's not much money, but it's more than all but three states pay to a family on welfare. The fifth day can be devoted to trying to get a job in the private sector. Poverty is not an act of God, but a lack of will on the part of policy-makers. Where people cannot read and write, get them into a program; test them for learning disabilities. Where people do not have a high school diploma, get them into a program where they can receive a GED, the equivalent of a diploma.

– Encourage congregations, civic groups, school associations, and others to participate in a massive assault on illiteracy in the nation.

– Encourage those same groups to build understanding and establish concrete goals by bringing people of differing faiths, races, and backgrounds together in homes for frank discussions.

– Cut the already enacted tax cut in half, and use the resources to invest in an improved nation. Modify the remaining half of the tax cut to benefit a broader cross-section of the tax-paying public.

71

– Face the eventual problems of Social Security retirement, which both parties are ducking. Recognize that real answers will not be popular. Forget investing Social Security funds in the stock market, a massively flawed temptation. However, to encourage investment by those with limited incomes, match up to one percent of the first $20,000 of income to people who use this to invest in the stock market or in long-term certificates of deposit.

Enacting any significant part of this program will require the interest and participation of many who now sit on the sidelines of public policy—including those who not only sit on the sidelines, but don't even pay attention to what is happening on the field.

FORMER UNIVERSITY OF CHICAGO president Robert Maynard Hutchins commented, "The death of democracy is not likely to be an assassination from ambush. It will be a slow extinction from apathy, indifference and undernourishment."[9]

Robert Putnam looks at our participation in community affairs and the results are not encouraging: "Between 1973 and 1994 the number of Americans who attended even one public meeting on town or school affairs...was cut by 40 percent....We now have sixteen million fewer participants in public meetings about local affairs, eight million fewer committee members, eight million fewer local organizational leaders, and three million fewer men and women organized to work for better government."[10] Much of this is because of less participation by younger people. Even more discouraging is this conclusion: "The declines are greatest among the better educated. Among the college educated, attendance at public meetings was nearly halved from 34 percent to 18 percent....Attendance at public meetings fell from 20 percent to 8 percent among those whose education ended in high school and from 7 percent to 3 percent among those who attended only elementary school."[11]

He notes the same trend in non-political civic groups. The PTA, for example, went from forty-seven members per hundred families with children under eighteen in 1959 to seventeen PTA members in 1981. One study concludes: "Between 1990 and 1997, the PTA lost half a million members, even though the number of families with children under eighteen grew by over 2 million and public school enrollment grew by over 5 million."[12]

Balancing that dismal picture a little is that, while people volunteer less for political campaigns and for organizations like the PTA, when service opportunities are well presented, volunteers do emerge. Habitat for Humanity, the volunteer organization that now builds 130,000 homes a year in this nation and in eighty-two other countries, has managed to capture approval and volunteers, thanks to a remarkable leader, Millard Fuller. For example, the largest student organization on the University of Michigan campus is Habitat for Humanity, with 457 members.

Professional organizations, like the American Bar Association, have increased membership because of great growth in numbers of attorneys and because of a belief by most lawyers that membership helps their income and adds a small prestige factor. Membership in labor unions has declined from approximately one-third of the work force to 13 percent.

In the field of religion, Putnam concludes: "The fraction of the population that spent any time on religion at all fell by nearly one-half [between 1965 and 1995]."[13] He attributes the change largely to a generational gap, with the younger adults much less inclined toward religious participation of any kind. However, he also notes that the percentage of those "intensely involved" has remained fairly constant.[14]

Putnam offers this important insight: Those who contribute to religious or other charitable organizations are much more likely to do voluntary community work, by a factor of 63 percent to 17 percent.[15]

We can find reasons—"excuses" is sometimes a better word—for our increasingly being disconnected from each other. A much higher percentage of women are employed full-time than a few decades ago, and men and women who are exhausted after working eight hours frequently are less inclined to use an evening to attend a PTA or church meeting. Crime in urban areas has caused increased fear of leaving home at night to attend a meeting of the Lions Club or Mothers Against Drunk Driving. But excuses, good or bad, don't build a better society. Isolation from others does not generate a sense of community, or an understanding of the problems that many in our society face. There is no simple formula for finding the proper balance between spending more time together as a family and participating in activities outside the household. Staying at home and watching television and saying to yourself that you are involved in a family activity is clearly not the proper answer. Parents also teach by example—primarily by example—and the example of participation or non-participation is likely to be followed in the years to come by their children.

WHEN I SEE THE INATTENTION by so many to the opportunities to influence our society, I recall scenes like:

- Speaking at the second anniversary of the bus boycott in Montgomery, Alabama, at the invitation of Martin Luther King Jr., and then spending two days with him and Ralph Abernathy and Rosa Parks and others, going from church to church telling people how to fill out the long forms that Alabama then required of African Americans before they could vote. How precious that vote seemed, and how many take it for granted today.

- Co-chairing with former president Jimmy Carter the international team monitoring the first free election in Liberia; getting up early in the morning on the day of election and before the polls opened he and I saw long—really long—lines of people waiting to cast their ballots.

- Being in Ghana before the country's first free election; meeting with candidates and the media, sensing the excitement that people had at doing something constructive for their nation and for their children.

- Heading an international team in Croatia when the late President Tudjman was up for reelection in a semi-free event, with everything from campaign laws to government-run television stacked against the opposition; four years later the country had a free election.

- Being in a small village in Bangladesh where women are "spreading their wings" for the first time through civic participation and in small businesses. One woman who had received a loan to buy a cow explained to us how that gave her income and independence.

All of these events had two things in common: the rights and liberties we in this country take for granted were not always there, and those citizens took seriously their ability to participate.

WHEN ABRAHAM LINCOLN and Stephen A. Douglas had their debates in the Illinois Senate race of 1858, thousands attended each verbal confrontation between the two. There was no public address system then, and no air conditioning. Poor roads and many other barriers made attendance inconvenient—but the public turned out in large numbers. Citizens discussed the issues among themselves after the debates.

One major factor—probably *the* major factor—that has changed our society since World War II is the intrusive presence of television in virtually every home. Most families have more than two television sets. TV captivates us and entertains us. It is so easy to find an excuse to stay home to watch a favorite show or the Monday night football game or even a video movie. What is worse—and even less social than watching television—is being mesmerized by the entertainment on a computer.

One of the nation's best-known comedians is Al Franken, who follows the political scene with keen interest and works in his zingers on social problems between our guffaws. Speaking of his father he writes: "He did spend time with me. Not necessarily quality time, but quantity time, hours and hours and hours of nonproductive, aimless quantity time. What did we do with this quantity time? Mainly, we watched television, hours and hours and hours of television."[16]

We became a great nation through citizen participation. Volunteering. The barriers to renewing that wholesome and vital habit are small, like watching television. A desirable change in conduct would take only a small amount of willpower. The rewards that each of us and our families could experience are huge compared with this one small investment. They are rewards far greater than anything the stock market can do for us.

My son Martin and his wife Julie permit their grade-school children to watch television only on weekends. My grandchildren are accustomed to that and I hear no objections from them. Are they harmed by this? I doubt it. Are they helped by it? I believe so. They are too young for us to know whether in later life this will translate into greater participation, but my sense is that if restraint on television watching continues, greater participation in other things will be part of their lives. My daughter Sheila and her husband Perry follow a somewhat similar practice with two older children. They receive few complaints from their children for the policy.

Tocqueville wrote: "How does it happen that in the United States, where the inhabitants have only recently immigrated to the land which they now occupy...everyone takes as zealous an interest in the affairs of his township, his county, and the whole state as if they were his own? It is because everyone...takes an active part in the government of society."[17]

If enough of us reverse our current habits of non-participation, we will again be building a better nation and a better world.

That may sound "pie-in-the-sky," but it's true.

CHAPTER SIX

EDUCATION

Human history becomes more and more a race between education and catastrophe.

—H. G. Wells, 1920[1]

We have not always been a nation that places a high premium on education, but we had the good fortune to have as our earliest leaders well-educated people. Gradually we came to see that increased educational opportunity would be good both for individuals and for our nation.

Today all candidates for public office claim to be strong supporters of education; it has the "motherhood and apple pie" aura to it. People want a good education for their children, though precisely how to get that is less clear to them, so, while candidates can easily make glorious speeches for education, following through in concrete terms is another matter. Because the public understanding of how to improve education is fuzzy, office-holders and candidates are generally able to get by with fuzzy responses when the real answers call for fundamental changes and sacrifice.

During our early years, the United States—like other nations — did not assume that everyone should be educated. The Constitution does not mention education, even though it touches on many other relatively minor matters. Education is barely mentioned in the debates at the 1787 Constitutional Convention. The men who wrote the Constitution favored education, in a general way, and Thomas Jefferson's detailed planning and enthusiasm for the University of Virginia had an impact on the fledgling nation of fewer than four million people. But a general public education for everyone as we have come to know it was not envisioned. However, before the Constitutional Convention met, John Adams wrote: "Laws for the liberal education of youth, especially for the lower classes of people, are so extremely wise and useful that to a humane and generous mind, no expense for this purpose would be thought extravagant."[2]

Most early education around the world had a religious orientation. The Egyptians and Sumerians (in the region of what is now Turkey) had a form of education as early as 3000 B.C. Students came from upper-class families and were taught by temple priests. Among the first to establish formal schools were the Chinese in the Han period (202 B.C. to 220 A.D.), during which education had a heavy Confucian emphasis. By the seventh century, Buddhism was exerting a strong influence on education. Movable type was first developed in China. The first book to use block printing, a Buddhist set of precepts, was produced in the year 868. Books assisted significantly in the education process. The city-state of Athens started an education system early in its history, but only the sons of Athenian citizens could attend, which excluded two-thirds of the boys, and all the girls. Rome followed Athens, and included a few girls as well as boys, but like other cultures, limited education to upper income people. Christian missionaries started schools in India in 1542, but the East India Company in British-ruled India provided education only for the children of the British occupiers. When England's William Wilberforce, known in the United States for his fight against slavery, tried to include in the charter of the East India Company a mandate to provide educational opportunities for the young people of India, his proposed amendment lost.

In the United States, New England led in education and Tocqueville noted that education is "the daughter of morality and religion.... Almost all education is entrusted to the clergy."[3] Harvard and Yale were founded primarily to provide an education for ministers. Harvard, named for Puritan minister John Harvard, taught medicine and law in addition to its primary focus on training the clergy. The father of John Adams sent his son to Harvard to become a minister, a path the future president did not follow. Yale also had a rigorous Puritan emphasis in its early years.

Generally during the first years in our country, as in other nations, only boys were educated. In the nation's first century there were "female seminaries" or academies, but only a few of them. In 1833, Oberlin College in Ohio became the country's first coeducational post-secondary school. No other institution followed that example until twenty years later when Antioch College, also in Ohio, was established. Cornell University in New York became the first eastern school to go coeducational, in 1872, almost a century after the founding of the nation. Even with our limitations, we were ahead of Europe in providing education for girls and young women. Tocqueville admired American leadership on this, but in one of the few cases where he misjudged events, he commented: "I am aware that an education [for females] is not without danger; I am sensible that it tends... to make cold and virtuous women instead of affectionate wives and agreeable companions to men."[4] Horizons gradually enlarged both in terms of who was taught and what was taught.

Our system of education evolved from the colonies and states, with little federal impact until the middle of the nineteenth century.

Parochial schools, primarily Catholic but also Lutheran, Dutch Reformed, and Jewish, pioneered grade school and high school education. Even more common, but totally without any national or regional structure, men and a few women who had been to high school or college offered to teach students for a fee, or parents got together and told someone that they would offer a certain amount for schooling. Typical of many who went into teaching, Elijah Lovejoy, later an anti-slavery newspaper editor and martyr to the cause of freedom, taught for one year in 1825 in the small town of China, Maine, after graduating from Waterville College (now

Colby College) in that state. He then joined the westward movement, set out for the frontier city of St. Louis, and started a one-room school, making enough income to send money to his parents in Maine and to buy a half-interest in the *St. Louis Times*.

This disorganized approach to education gradually yielded to states providing elementary education and eventually the opportunity for a high school education. Massachusetts passed a compulsory school attendance law in 1852. Several states set aside acreage in each township to be used for educational purposes.

Not until 1975 did the nation resolve to provide education for all young people with disabilities through a congressional act signed into law by President Gerald Ford. We are improving our performance, but progress is slow.

SHORTLY BEFORE LEAVING the Senate, I visited eighteen public schools on the south and west side of Chicago, the poorer areas of the city. I took no reporters with me.

I learned that leadership makes a huge difference. The new chancellor of the New York City Department of Education, Joel Klein, has wisely decided to initiate academies to train principals in doing effective work. The person who is a good teacher is not necessarily a good administrator and leader, but can be if properly trained.

In one school on the dismal west side of Chicago, I walked in expecting to be depressed. The principal, Dr. Arletta Holloway, an African American, had the students excited and the teachers excited. She brought in parents regularly, not only to visit the classrooms but also to learn basic literacy skills. That school is the pride of the neighborhood, and many of its students will do well in the future.

I visited another school and within five minutes the principal said to me, "These students don't have much potential." I could feel that attitude permeating everything from the dull hallways to the work of the teachers. Whatever potential those students may have will be achieved despite that school—not because of it.

Even excellent leadership cannot make up for deficiencies in impoverished areas. A 2001 study of teachers from the seventh through the twelfth grades in Illinois public schools found: "Fifty percent of those in high-poverty schools had teachers who admitted they did not have [even] minors in the fields they were teaching compared to 13 percent in low-poverty schools."[5]

THE UNITED STATES cannot accurately be described as a leader in pre-college education. No nation has copied our approaches to grade and high school education.

However, in higher education we are acknowledged to be the leader. That is progress from where we once stood. While Tocqueville does not mention higher education, he makes an observation that reflects its status in 1831: "It must be acknowledged that in few of the civilized nations of our time have the higher sciences made less progress than in the United States; and in few have great artists, distinguished poets, or celebrated writers been more rare."[6] That would soon change.

Two significant actions by the federal government had a powerful influence in awakening Americans to the advantages of higher education.

The first was the Land Grant Act of 1862, introduced by Congressman Justin Smith Morrill of Vermont—later a senator—and signed into law by Abraham Lincoln. It was a measure that had been vetoed by Lincoln's weak predecessor, President James Buchanan. That act gave states thirty thousand acres for each member of Congress, with the profit from the sale of the lands to be used for establishing colleges that would teach "agriculture and the mechanical arts," from which many got the name "A and M" colleges and universities. Schools could teach other subjects and did. The act gave a huge thrust forward to higher education and indirectly to the elementary and high schools that had to prepare the future college students. Approximately one-fifth of the college degrees granted today are from those schools. These universities tended to be among the first to admit women. Because they were state-run schools and had federal assistance, they charged less and made college open to many more students.

However, a post-secondary education remained an opportunity for only a small minority of the population until legislation passed at the end of World War II known as the GI Bill, which paid the tuition and living costs for veterans to go to college. Many who had not finished high school either completed the work or were conditionally admitted to colleges, permitted to remain only if they could compete academically at the college level, and most did.

It gave the nation's economy a huge lift and put greater stress on education at all levels. Other federal college grant and loan programs then passed Congress. Completing high school and going to college no longer remained a dream exclusively for the elite.

The accessibility of college to all thrust the United States into economic leadership as well as leadership in post-secondary education. Many nations have studied our pioneering in the college field, though most countries do not have financial resources like ours to make the opportunity for college available to all their people.

However, we still have problems with college education in the United States. In the years immediately after World War II federal aid to students was approximately three-fourths in the form of grants, one-fourth in the form of loans. That has reversed itself to three-fourths loans and one-fourth grants. Many students now leave college with heavy loan burdens, postponing the day when they can have a home and family. Decisions about what to study are frequently distorted by the fact that certain professions make it easier to repay loans. The GI Bill for veterans paid full tuition to the school of choice—Harvard or a state university—but today students from low-income families are increasingly faced with the reality that the so-called elite schools are beyond their reach, further segregating our society on an economic basis.

Worst of all, taking on a sizable loan presents a huge barrier to even going to college for many low-income families who struggle to find food and shelter and cannot imagine carrying a loan burden of $20,000 to $30,000 or more. The federal Advisory Committee on

Student Financial Assistance reported that in the decade of the 1990s two million qualified high school graduates who could have benefited from a college education did not attend, almost all for financial reasons—a huge loss to the nation's economy. In 1999–2000, 71 percent of students from families with income of less than $20,000 graduated with debt. Student loan authorities describe college loan repayments as "unmanageable" if they exceed 8 percent of income. That is the status of 55 percent of African Americans after their academic years, and of 58 percent of Hispanic Americans.[7] The National Center for Public Policy and Higher Education reports: "Our conclusion regarding the affordability of a college or university education is this: Americans are losing ground."[8] They note that "only the wealthiest families have seen their incomes keep pace with increases in tuition."[9] The share of average family income required to pay tuition at a four-year public institution has risen from 12 percent in 1980 to 24 percent in 2000, and at four-year private schools from 57 percent to 116 percent.

Society's attitude toward those teaching in higher education has not always been positive. There is resentment to a perceived elitism, and the attitude by academics too often has been aloofness from our society's ills. In an election-year debate, Senator James Buckley referred to his opponent and the eventual victor as "Professor [Daniel] Moynihan." Moynihan's rejoinder: "I knew this campaign would get dirty."[10] One of the nation's premier educators, Vartan Gregorian, accurately observed: "Education has been shunted aside, not institutionally but intellectually. We have not involved our educational leaders, and we have not galvanized their efforts on behalf of the nation."[11] Leaders in higher education, like their counterparts in religion, too often have not wanted to "dirty their hands" in politics—quite a shift from Plato's attitude in his academy. Only a few decades ago, for example, the University of Illinois would not let a presidential candidate or any other candidate who did not hold the office he or she sought speak on the campus.

It became apparent in late 2001 that Illinois and almost all the states faced budget crunches, and that higher education could receive substantial cuts, not good for the universities or their communities, but most important, not good for our state and nation.

I suggested to a few leaders on the campus on which I am located, Southern Illinois University, and to three or four leaders on other campuses that the faculty around the state should organize politically, show evidence of political involvement to the two candidates for governor, and press for commitments to see that our state leads in higher education; this would be a winner for everyone. The idea didn't catch fire. I told them that with my heavy schedule I couldn't commit much time to such an effort, but I would try to help. So far as I know nothing ever happened. After the election, Illinois along with most states faced a financial squeeze and higher education suffered. Faculty groups around the state passed resolutions condemning the cuts, but by then the period of helping to shape policy had passed.

"Right makes might" is a great motto, but it is true only if those in the right really work at it. I should have done more. Looking around me I realize that people who are extremely articulate in their sphere of expertise are sometimes not sophisticated in using the tools of democracy to bring about change. How this is rectified I am not sure, but I know that faculty members who don't handle the tools of public life well are not likely to convey the values of leadership and participation to their students. Why don't students take more of an interest in political life? I learned part of the answer.

One of the great deficiencies in education is not conveying a sense of civic responsibility. Eugene Lang, a remarkable and creative philanthropist in New York City, is trying to do this, starting with a small number of colleges and making modest changes in the curriculum. He correctly believes, for example, that students can be enriched educationally and become better citizens if they engage in practical, voluntary service working with people who need help. He likes teaching "civics," an almost outdated term in practice but not in need. He calls his effort Project Pericles, quoting from Pericles's remarkable funeral tribute to Thucydides about what a democracy should be.

Having a sense of American history, where we have been, what we stand for, somehow bypasses too many at all levels of education. Political observer David Gergen, while fully aware of Richard Nixon's flaws, wrote that "his capacity to see the road behind enabled him to see where the road was heading. It is a priceless asset for a leader.... His capacity as a visionary exceeds that of other presidents in modern times and was squarely based upon his understanding of history.... It is surprising that few politicians appreciate how much a capacity to speak knowledgeably from history can enhance the stature of a leader."[12]

I came into Congress right after the Nixon presidency and had no contact with him until I entered the Senate. I followed his interviews on foreign policy and I found, a little to my surprise, depth and wisdom in Nixon's views. I had limited contact with him then, not enough to judge the validity of David Gergen's comments about his understanding of history. But I believe Gergen was right. One of Harry Truman's great strengths as president was his knowledge of history and his sense of history. Lincoln also had both qualities.

As Vartan Gregorian observes, we have two things—one good, one bad—happening: The good is the explosion of knowledge through the Internet, and a growth in new book titles to approximately 850,000 annually, with the United States accounting for 75,000 of these; we published approximately 10,000 a few decades ago. The bad news is that we are specializing so much that we have created a "fragmentation of knowledge."[13]

In the college years, if not before, students should accumulate an understanding of where we have come as a nation, and at least a little comprehension of the rest of the world along with a view of history that is not solely focused on the U.S. and Western Europe.

However, our major educational deficiencies remain at the pre-college level.

We are the only nation in which students can attend grade school, high school, and college, get a Ph.D., and never have a year of a foreign language. It is one of the reasons—although not the only one—for our insularity. Visitors from other nations are often appalled at our lack of knowledge of and insensitivity to the rest of the world.

After being named ambassador to Indonesia, one of this nation's most thoughtful foreign policy experts, David Newsom, wrote to the State Department about talks he would hold with developing nations on key resource questions: "On the basis of a number of discussions with recent visitors from the United States, there seems to be an insufficient public understanding of the historical background and atmosphere in which we must conduct these discussions."[14] He wrote that in 1974. Things have not improved since then, despite the fact that the percentage of those graduating from high school has doubled since 1960 and grown by one-third since 1974.

A group called the Institute for American Values, primarily composed of academic leaders, issued a statement that includes this sentence: "We recognize that at times our nation has acted with arrogance and ignorance toward other societies."[15] Responsibility for much of the ignorance must be laid at the feet of American education at all levels.

Elementary and secondary students in Singapore attend school 280 days a year, in Japan 243, in Germany 240—the list goes on. In the United States we average less than 180 days a year. Why? In theory, so that our children can go out and harvest the crops. That work is no longer required even in rural America. A high school student in Japan graduates with more hours in the classroom than a college graduate in the United States. If our children are to be competitive with the rest of the world, that will have to change.

There is a serious gap in educational opportunity for those who are poor. The comparison of the public schools in the middle and upper income areas of our nation with the impoverished rural and inner city regions is stark. Much of the reason for poverty in those areas is that we have not paid attention to adult illiteracy or limited literacy. Income goes up and unemployment goes down as the education level rises. Unemployment rates for people without a high school diploma are about 13 percent, for high school graduates 6 percent, for those with some college education 4 percent, and for college graduates under 3 percent. Illiterate—or near-illiterate—people do not earn much. People who are illiterate are much less likely to vote, engage in any form of civic activity, attend church, or go to a child's school to meet a teacher or learn about the school. Their overwhelming feeling of inadequacy usually prevents them from being more than barely productive; it also prevents them from enriching the lives of their children at home through books and reading. Because of limited income, healthy meals and decent housing and visits to a physician or dentist are less likely for their children. Such deficiencies have long-term consequences.

These families are more likely to use TV as a baby-sitter.

Green Bay football coach Vince Lombardi is supposed to have said: "Winning is a habit, but unfortunately so is losing." The illiterate and near-illiterate in our society are accustomed to losing and are likely to pass that attitude on to their children unless the pattern is broken.

Compounding this is the economic segregation of our society, noted in chapter 3. Except for people in small towns, wherever we live our neighbors are roughly in the same income category. We have been segregating ourselves not only by the dollars we earn, but also—because of illiteracy—by educational attainment. Too often the poor have no books in their homes; neither do their neighbors. Neighborhoods with low literacy rates, low educational attainment, are also places with high unemployment, high crime rates, high drug use, and high alcoholism.

Intensified pre-school and in-school individual attention efforts are helping a scattered few living in these circumstances, but their numbers remain too small.

Bright spots in some of these neighborhoods are parochial schools, primarily—but not always—Roman Catholic. The majority of students served in most of the inner city Catholic schools are not Catholic by affiliation. The education provided in almost all cases is clearly superior to that of neighboring public schools. Parochial schools enjoy the luxury of picking which students to accept and of discharging or suspending those who do not follow strict school discipline. As a society we are struggling with how we can both take advantage of these schools, learn from them, yet not get too enmeshed in church-state complexities.

The U.S. Supreme Court ruled 5-4 that school vouchers to parents can be granted constitutionally. But what is constitutional is not always wise. At the college level we permit students to choose among private or public schools. That has worked well. The assumption is that at the college level there is a degree of maturity so that the student can accept or reject the religious orientation of the college without difficulty, that there is no "excessive entanglement" of church and state (the key phrase for the U.S. Supreme Court for decades). At the third-grade level, however, the opportunities for religious inculcation are greater, and not just in Catholic schools but in other schools that might emerge, schools that could be run by religious extremists. At the same time, should we deny a third grader the chance for a quality education because of concerns for what might be taught in the name of religion?

Proponents ask: Why shouldn't parents have the choice to send children, along with tax subsidies, to private schools as we do at the college level? Opponents argue there is no diversity of choice at elementary and high schools as there is at the college level, and that the government would run the risk of being involved in indoctrination for a small group of religions.

Several states are now dealing with this church-state quagmire and it is likely that practical lessons can be learned. At the federal level, assistance to pre-college education is so low, about 6 percent of the cost, that diluting those sums further is not likely. The advantage of having fifty states is that we have fifty laboratories in which we can experiment with vouchers. My guess is that we will have failures, but we will also have successes that eventually can benefit the nation.

CHAPTER SEVEN

OPTIMISM

The outstanding characteristic of America is the refusal of Americans to accept defects in their society as irremediable.

—Lewis Galantiere, 1954[1]

The leaders who broke from the British and thought they could create a sensible system of self-government were optimists, literally risking their necks to try this experiment which we call America.

It was not only the leaders. People took a dangerous voyage by ship across the Atlantic in those early days, believing that they could better themselves and their families. Often their neighbors in the countries from which they came seriously questioned not only their judgment but sometimes their sanity.

Whether the initial motivation for traveling to this unknown world was religious or economic or political—or simply adventure—they had a basic optimism. Optimists are the people who change the world. Those who give up never will.

I cannot imagine a basketball coach starting his first session with a new team by saying, "We're probably not going to have a good season." Being successful requires a certain level of hope and optimism. As I worked on this chapter, I received a phone call from someone who believes a change in the law on teacher certification is desirable. I suggested that he write to his state legislators and the Illinois Board of Education with his recommendations. "They won't listen to me," he responded. I told him that they certainly won't listen to him if he doesn't contact them. A minimal level of belief that you may be able to effect change is essential to achieving it.

When I speak to a university audience, I usually follow up with a question and answer period. After I've made my policy recommendations there is sometimes a faculty member—usually a young faculty member—who stands up and says, "That won't work because..." He then recites all the things that are wrong with the policy-making process. My response: "For every reason you give me for cynicism, I can give you ten more. But the cynics aren't going to build a better world. We need people like you working to achieve change, not telling us why it can't be happen."

In no small part because of the optimism and hope of those who founded our nation, democracy is slowly but certainly spreading around the world. Even the harshest dictatorship, North Korea, has the trappings of democracy. North Koreans feel compelled to have a parliament, a "rubber stamp" body to be sure, but the fact that they have one is a recognition of the power and the pull of democracy. And occasionally—Serbia is an example—those docile and compliant trappings of democracy take on real significance. Iran's ruling religious elite were stunned when citizens unexpectedly elected a moderate as president (with limited power) and a moderate parliament. In speaking of another region, *The Economist* notes: "Despite what most outsiders think, Africa is becoming more democratic."[2] President Jimmy Carter's exhortations about democracy and human rights helped change the map of Latin America so that only one dictatorship remains in that region. Cynics said of almost every nation and region infested by dictatorships, "Democracy won't work there." Generally they have been proven wrong.

There always are "prophets of gloom and doom," but even our leaders of more somber mood, with Abraham Lincoln being a prime example, were able to radiate hope. When Lincoln won an election, his statements did not reflect elation. When Stephen A. Douglas lost to Lincoln, Douglas sounded a victorious note. Lincoln's first election race, which he lost, took place when he was a twenty-three-year old candidate for state representative. He concluded his brief candidacy announcement to the newspaper: "If the good people in their wisdom shall see fit to keep me in the background, I have been too familiar with disappointments to be very much chagrined."[3] Yet this somewhat dour figure believed he could hold the Union together and also rid this nation of the plague of slavery—and he did both. His melancholy moods did not prevent him from believing he could change things for the better.

Winston Churchill, whose mother was an American, led the British after the Nazis had conquered the rest of western Europe. In the midst of enemy poundings of his country from the air—and one month before the United States entered the fray—he told a school group: "These are not dark days; these are great days—the greatest days our country has ever lived."[4] His optimism breathed hope into a people suffering heavy casualties.

When people approached President Thomas Jefferson with the idea of the Louisiana Purchase, he could have said to himself, "What will we do with all that territory? It will require federal expenditures to govern it. People will criticize me for this waste of taxpayers' dollars." Instead, Jefferson, who had realistic dreams and a spirit of hope and optimism, moved ahead with what ultimately was of immense importance to our nation's future. Our country purchased what became all or part of fifteen states, at three cents per acre. It is clear now that Jefferson acted wisely, although this was not obvious to everyone then. Jefferson originally wanted to purchase only New Orleans. The total cost to the United States for the entire territory was $15 million. The decision caused considerable debate in the Senate, which had to approve it because it took the form of a treaty with France. The Senate finally acted favorably by a vote of 24 to 7.

Another matter of controversy involved William Seward, secretary of state under Abraham Lincoln and President Andrew

Johnson. In 1867 the United States had the opportunity to purchase Alaska from Russia for $7,200,000. Seward created great controversy by pushing for it. It became known as "Seward's Folly"—and turned out to be a great investment.

Every nation, every state, every community and university and school needs people of vision and hope who are willing to risk criticism to achieve noble ends. The pessimists and nay-sayers who sit on the sidelines and dissect and nitpick and disapprove should be listened to—but not too much.

MEN AND WOMEN get into politics either because they like the recognition—they enjoy being called "Senator" or "Governor" or "Mr. President"—or they get into politics because they believe they can effect constructive change. The latter requires optimism, a belief that you can bring about improvements in our society.

One of the major hurdles in helping people out of poverty, people who have been enmeshed in that depressed economic state for several years or even generations, is to give them a sense of hope, a sense that they really can change their lives. People who have given up are difficult to help. Whatever anti-poverty programs are tried, the most important ingredient is one that has no cost: hope.

It is not only the impoverished who need hope. We could change things if enough citizens and policymakers really understood that poverty is not an act of God, some permanent blight or birthmark people have, but a temporary condition that becomes permanent only if the non-poor acquiesce and believe that poverty cannot be virtually eliminated and the poor join them in that belief. Would we all be richer if we fairly dramatically reduced poverty within our nation and around the world? To ask the question is to answer it. Reducing poverty will require a temporary small sacrifice on the part of many of us—with big payoffs in the long run—but the big barrier is not the dollars but the will, which comes from the belief that real change can be effected. The sacrifice required is not simply a relatively few tax dollars, but making the time to write to legislators, to attend meetings, to have meaningful contact with people who struggle. One of the traditional seven deadly sins is sloth, laziness. It is more of a threat to our doing something for those who are economically devastated than is the call for spending money to give them the opportunity to better themselves.

A COMMUNITY IN SOUTHERN ILLINOIS that faced—and continues to face—serious economic problems asked me if I could help. I told them to get their Rotary Club, Woman's Club, and a few other groups together on a night we agreed upon. I then asked an imaginative man from our region who had built a large travel agency from scratch and two business leaders from Chicago to spend half a day visiting and getting acquainted with the area so that in the evening we would get together and present their ideas to the groups at a dinner meeting. They presented their suggestions. In the discussion on each idea, someone in the audience would say, "That won't work here because..." Of course, if you believe something won't work, it won't. I had wasted everyone's time. If someone in the audience had stood up and said, "That's a great idea," and then suggested they get six people together to work on it, something could have been achieved. I am sure that people in that community today are blaming everyone but themselves for their problems.

I am an optimist by nature. But let me tell you of a time when I let myself—and perhaps thousands of other people—down. In 1994 word filtered through to us and the rest of the world that large numbers of people were being slaughtered in Rwanda in Africa because of ethnic strife. Eventually approximately eight hundred thousand Rwandans were killed. I got on the phone to Canadian General Romeo Dallaire, who was in charge of a small contingent of UN troops in the capital city of Kigali. Senator James Jeffords of Vermont joined me on the phone. General Dallaire told us that if he could get five to eight thousand troops quickly, he could stop the mass murders. Jim Jeffords and I had a letter hand-delivered to the White House that day, urging that a Security Council meeting of the UN be called immediately to authorize the troop deployment. We added that if the United States was unwilling to provide troops, we should at least provide transportation.

I did not hear anything for several days and, when I called the White House, I received this response: "There just isn't a base of public support for doing anything in Africa." It was a tragically anemic response. I had previously introduced a resolution urging attention to what was happening and it had met with indifference from my Senate colleagues and opposition from the administration. After the White House rejection I should have called a press conference, even though reporters might not have shown up. Senator George Mitchell's successful negotiation in Northern Ireland—a region for which there is some public interest in this country—generated one television camera when he came back to the United States to report.

I knew there was little media or public interest in Africa, but I should have tried calling a press conference and urged reporters to come. I could have called religious leaders in the nation, encouraging them to get involved. Instead, disheartened by the indifference of people in the Senate and in the White House who should have responded, I gave up. I should not have. Would it have made a difference? Probably not, but it might have, and giving up was a dishonorable exit.

I cannot think of anyone in any field of endeavor who takes a risk without having a spirit of optimism, of hope. I'm writing this book with the belief that at least a few people who read it will be turned on and dedicate themselves to constructive activity. I risk my time. My publisher, Orbis Books, believes that people will buy the book and that it will help to serve the compassionate mission of Maryknoll, which is the financial and inspirational backbone of Orbis.

An automobile mechanic takes my car and is optimistic that he can fix it. People who are blessed with children—even disabled children—see the good that can come from helping them. Author and inspirer Elie Wiesel uses the devastating experience of the Holocaust to lift us to do noble things, believing that humanity can be motivated to do good as well as evil.

Jonas Salk, who developed the polio vaccine, worked eight years before he found a formula that worked and that the U.S. government approved. Failure after failure in his research did not stop him. He had a sense that by working with others he could contain this terrible scourge. He radiated optimism.

America has no monopoly on optimism, but it is more a part of our culture and our heritage than it is in many other nations. Worthy goals are not achieved easily. But unless there is a spirit of hope, of optimism, no individual or community or university or state or nation will achieve truly constructive aims.

However, optimism needs to be aimed at specific goals. A cheery, pleasant, unfocused optimism will make a person more likeable, but does not accomplish anything. A focused optimism caused people to get into ships and migrate to the United States. A focused optimism resulted in the discovery of the smallpox vaccine. Optimism needs to be applied.

I HAVE DONE A LITTLE WORK on the world's water problems. We will come close to doubling the world's population in the next fifty to ninety years, depending on whose projection you accept. But, while the population mark on a chart is going through the roof, our water supply is constant, a flat line. When I first started to sense the dimensions of the problem, I asked my staff to assemble a few water experts who, among other things, could advise me on where we should go in finding less expensive ways of converting salt water to fresh water, an old dream of Presidents Dwight Eisenhower and John F. Kennedy. Approximately 97 percent of the earth's water is salt water, and two-thirds of the remaining 3 percent is tied up in icebergs and snow. So we are living on 1 percent of the earth's water. It is obvious to me—though not to everyone—that we will have to tap into the 97 percent as quickly as possible if we are to avoid wars over water as well as terrible nutrition problems. Seventy percent of the world's population lives within fifty miles of the ocean.

My staff pulled together four or five knowledgeable people from around the nation and when we talked one evening about desalinated water they assured me that it could never be produced inexpensively enough and in sufficient quantities to ever make a difference. I had one meeting with them. I could see that they were able people, but they didn't believe desalination would ever amount to anything. This was the conventional viewpoint. I told my staff, "I want another meeting with a different group. I don't want to hear from people who say it can't be done. I want to meet with people who believe that it can, who believe we can find the answers."

I had a much better second meeting! And we are making progress. Not as rapidly as I would like, but from the scientific community to the leaders of governments around the world, there is a slowly growing realization that desalination is a major part of our long-term answer.

In every community, on every campus, in every state, in every nation, on every issue there are the non-dreamers, the nay-sayers who find all the "practical" reasons why real change for the better is not possible. Treat them politely. They do a little harm, but not much. Just don't let them set the course for a community or campus or state or nation.

They are as much a part of the United States as the rest of us, but they are the ones who would have stayed at home rather than venture to the new frontier across the Atlantic Ocean. Founded by creative but practical optimists, America should not be trapped by the pseudo-sophisticated cynics who will not build a better world.

CHAPTER EIGHT

RESPECT FOR THE LAW

If you want peace, work for justice.
—Pope Paul VI

We are an inconsistent people on the law. Drive down a highway posted at 55 miles per hour maximum and a stream of cars will pass you. But if the president of the United States clearly violates a significant provision of the law, he (eventually she) will face serious consequences, at the least terrible public relations.

During my Army service shortly after the end of World War II, I was stationed in Germany and the heavy-smoking Germans were desperate for American cigarettes. Each American GI got an allotment of cigarettes, whether we smoked or not, and the illegal black market sale of American cigarettes by GIs was massive. (I noticed that those who sold cigarettes illegally saw no inconsistency in complaining about crooked politicians.) Enforcing the black market regulation would have been extremely unpopular, both with our troops and with the Germans. As we started overseas in a troop ship, the top officers told us the ship rules, one of which prohibited playing poker for money. At least one-third of the bored soldiers openly violated that rule, and when officers walked through the mass of enlisted men congregated on the deck for fresh air, those officers somehow didn't see the card games going on all around them. When the nation outlawed the sale of alcoholic drinks, one Nevada mayor threatened to put "a barrel of whiskey with a dipper" on every street corner, much to the delight of his constituents.[1]

In times of national emergency, disregard for the law and for the rights of others can become dangerous. Whether fighting Nazis during World War II or terrorists today, we must remember what we stand for as well as what we oppose. Taking 115,000 Japanese Americans from California, Oregon and Washington during World War II—not one of whom had committed a crime—and sending them off to camps had immense popularity in the patriotic fervor of 1942. It is a stain on the record of our nation. Today, because of the terrorist threat, people have been imprisoned without having been given the right to see a lawyer. There have been other compromises of basic freedoms—the types of unnecessary moves we historically take in every national emergency—steps that we will look upon later with embarrassment. We say we are in "a war against terrorism" and because of that hold more than six hundred prisoners at the U.S. military base in Guantanamo, Cuba. On the other hand, claiming that this is not actually a war, we will not release the names nor the countries of origin of these prisoners. Neither will we give them any other rights accorded prisoners of war under the Geneva Convention which we signed. Twenty-seven of those held at Guantanamo have attempted suicide.

During the anti-immigrant fervor a few years before September 11th, a 1996 bill (which I voted against) gave sweeping and arbitrary powers to the Immigration and Naturalization Service (I.N.S.). The director of the Jesuit Refugee Service reported in 2001 that the agency "now holds over 20,000 noncitizens in detention every day—more than three times the 1996 number."[2] The Supreme Court limited the ability of I.N.S. to do this in two decisions prior to September 11th, but no one knows where the Supreme Court and the Justice Department will go in the fervor of today's climate.

Ten weeks after the terrorist attack on New York City, the Associated Press carried this story:

> Attorney General John Ashcroft said that nearly 1,200 have been arrested or detained in the investigation that followed the September 11 attacks.... The names of those charged will not be released. Part of the rationale for not releasing the names of those in custody, Ashcroft said, is to keep Bin Laden from knowing who is in custody.[3]

That is thin ice for an official of a free government to stand on! We also don't know how many were detained for lengthy periods before their families were informed or how many were denied the right to counsel.

On many campuses during the Vietnam War defenders of the war would be hackled with catcalls and so much noise from an audience that they could not speak. I am sure those students thought they were fighting for the patriotic, anti-war effort. In fact, they were hurting their cause as well as denying the right to free speech to people who should have been heard. Years after the Vietnam War, Senator George McGovern, a strong foe of the war, said we would have pulled out of Vietnam sooner but for the lack of restraint on the part of some of the war's opponents. One anti-Vietnam protester years later recalled, "I was so certain that I was right that I was dangerous."[4]

When the publisher of the *Sacramento Bee*, Janis Besler Heaphy, spoke at a college commencement after September 11th and questioned the civil liberties aspects of the U.S. government's response, a rowdy audience prevented her from finishing her remarks. They were *not* being patriotic. Patriotism is not simply waving a flag; it is also defending our basic freedoms, including the right of free speech. That implies giving others the right to listen. A few months after this incident, Vice President Richard Cheney spoke in San Francisco and hecklers stopped his talk, believing that they were helping their cause, but actually harming it—and harming our system. There are peaceful, nondisruptive ways of protesting the views of a speaker.

At West Brook High School in Beaumont, Texas, valedictorian Joanna Li's planned remarks included these words: "Have you noticed now that you're graduating, everyone has advice to give you? Work hard. Don't forget who you really are. Persevere. Remember your priorities. The truth is out there. That's all good and well ... but they seem to forget one important thing.... Have fun."[5] The school administration prevented her from saying that. A small thing, but the small victories or defeats for freedom add up.

INCONSISTENCY IN ATTITUDES toward the law is found in nations as well as in individuals. Those who founded our nation showed a remarkable reverence for the law, yet so massively broke the law under which they operated in the colonies that the British considered them traitors. Respect for the law, but not idolatry of the law, has been part of the U.S. scene from the days that preceded our nationhood. During World War II we properly criticized those in Germany who followed legal orders and massacred almost the entire Jewish population in that country. After that war, international trials held in Germany, led by the U.S., found those who obeyed Hitler's laws guilty, and a few leaders were executed. We recognized that there is a law of morality higher than written statutes.

IT IS IRONIC THAT IN 2002 an International Criminal Court became a reality, even though the United States opposed its creation. We headed the effort to bring to trial the Nazi leaders after World War II; we offered rewards for the capture of Serbian leaders in the recent Yugoslav conflict. Then we refuse to participate in concrete, long-term action for justice, saying that we would not want our armed service personnel tried by an international court. The reality is that any country that is willing to try its own people for humanitarian abuses does not have to worry. But despite that clear part of the authorization of the International Criminal Court, the

United States joined with most dictators in opposing its creation, while almost all the world's democracies approved and created the court. We cannot expect esteem from others if we say the law is good for them, but not for us.

During the civil rights struggles of the 1950s and 1960s, Martin Luther King Jr. advocated peaceful violation of the segregation statutes and a willingness to be arrested for the violation of laws that had as their base an immoral premise. In June 1956, Alabama outlawed the National Association for the Advancement of Colored People (NAACP), a clearly unconstitutional action eventually overthrown by the courts. But the law gained state-wide and national publicity, and within two weeks the Alabama Christian Movement for Human Rights was formed to continue the challenging work of the NAACP. If that new group had been outlawed, another organization with the same aims would have formed quickly. Using the law to impede the cause of justice cannot work in the long term in a free society. However, the words in the law books do not live in isolation from our culture. Martin Luther King Jr. understood that, and with his movement in Montgomery, Alabama, less than two years old, he stressed over and over the need to avoid reciprocating hatred with hatred. He told a gathering at his Dexter Avenue Baptist Church: "We've got to revolt in such a way that after [the] revolt is over we can live with people as their brothers and their sisters. Our aim must never be to defeat them or humiliate them."[6]

"No one is above the law," we hear repeatedly, and generally that is true. We have a tradition of reverence for the law. As Tocqueville noted: "The American submits without a murmur to the authority of the pettiest magistrate."[7]

We have penalties for violation of the law. The administration of justice is not perfect; we have much room for improvement. But it is more true in our nation than in many countries that high position or wealth does not exempt from the provisions of the law. Senators and governors and judges and cabinet members and millionaires have been imprisoned. Any citizen or member of Congress can say, "The president should be impeached," without fear of being imprisoned for that statement, and undoubtedly at least a few have said that under every presidency. Shouting "Impeach the president" and having a genuine cause for the action are two strikingly different things.

President Andrew Johnson came within one vote of being tossed out of office. President Richard Nixon would have been removed had he not resigned. President Bill Clinton went through an impeachment trial in the Senate after the House voted to bring him before the Senate for removal from office, but the Senate did not vote to take the presidency from him. In these three cases, the action of Congress reminded all Americans, as well as people in other nations, of the limitations of power in the United States.

That does not mean that the administration of justice is always what it should be. There are at least four major areas where living the ideals of the nation's founders can be improved.

Discrimination in the Application of the Criminal Law

If you are an African American brought before the courts, you are more likely to be found guilty and sentenced to prison than if you are white. The same is true for Latinos, and in some areas of the country for American Indians. Part of the reason for this is prejudice of jurors or judges or prosecutors. The problem is also that these minorities who often are impoverished are the least likely to afford a good attorney, and so a court-appointed lawyer represents the defendant, perhaps with another hundred cases he or she is handling. Even prejudice by that counsel may be a factor in what ultimately happens.

The Justice Department reported that in the year 2000, 13 percent of our population was African American, 14 percent of drug users were African American, and 56 percent of those sentenced to prisons and jails for drug offenses hailed from that minority. Among youthful offenders, 26 percent of those arrested in 1998 were African American and 58 percent of those sentenced to state prisons fall into that category.[8]

102

Studies in New Jersey and elsewhere show that an African American male is much more likely to be stopped for a traffic offense than his white counterpart.

The most casual student of this field recognizes the problem. How to deal with it is more difficult. At the very least, officers of the court and law enforcement officials should be educated in seminars about the nature of this barrier to justice. Unfortunately, however, the barrier will linger with us as long as prejudices sully our society.

Percentages of minorities hide the vastness of total numbers. We have far more people in prisons and jails per 100,000 citizens than any other nation. We have slightly more than 2,000,000 in our prisons, 4,000,000 on probation, and 750,000 on parole from prisons. These are astounding numbers by themselves, but they are galling numbers for many in minority communities who recognize the discriminatory application of the law. Crime authority Marc Mauer writes: "No other society in human history has ever imprisoned so many of its own citizens for the purposes of crime control."[9] We are 4 percent of the world's population and have 25 percent of its prisoners. As of 2002, we had 702 prisoners per 100,000 population. The highest number in Western Europe is Portugal with 131. Finland has 52—7 percent of our figure.

Failure to Make Prisons Places of Rehabilitation

Roughly 81 percent of those in our prisons and jails are high school dropouts, a high percentage of whom cannot read a newspaper. When Tocqueville visited the United States, he came to look at our enlightened policies in handling those sentenced for criminal acts. Today people visit the United States to see an example of how *not* to handle those convicted of criminal offenses.

Education in many prisons and jails is almost non-existent. Yet we know that the more education someone incarcerated has, the less likely that person is to return to prison.

Columnist Clarence Page has an insightful observation:

103

I once met with a group of ex-convicts, almost all of whom happened to be black like me....I asked each of them to think back to when they were kids and tell me what they wanted to be.

"A lawyer," said one.

"A carpenter," said another.

"A railroad engineer," said another.

None of them said they wanted to be gangsters.

It's the same with kids today. Ask them what they want to be when they grow up and you are probably not going to hear: "I want to be a thug."[10]

Most people in prisons and jails are there for drug offenses or drug-related offenses, like a burglary in order to pay for drugs. Most of those prisoners do *not* get drug rehabilitation assistance while incarcerated and few do after release.

The economic costs for imprisoning a higher percentage of our population than any other nation are staggering, and the human costs even greater.

Those in our prisons and jails who have learning disabilities generally get no assessment. They frequently have no inkling that their problem is not stupidity but a quirk in how their brain operates. If there is no assessment, there is no assistance.

Roughly one-fourth of those in prisons and jails today have mental problems. No one knows the figure with precision. These men and women in an earlier period would have been in mental hospitals. In our understandable zeal to avoid warehousing people in state mental hospitals, we reduced those numbers from six hundred thousand to fifty thousand, assuming that community mental health facilities would be available. In most cases they have not been created. Even where they exist, people with mental problems who do not have someone to steer them regularly to such a facility, or get them to take a helpful drug regularly, get lost. They cannot function well enough to show up for a Tuesday appointment or to take their medicine regularly. They end up as street people, or in prisons and jails. Many go in and out of local jails several times a year. This is an expensive form of non-treatment of mental illness. A 2002 federal government report notes: "Studies demonstrate that approximately one third of male detainees and one quarter of female detainees who needed services for severe mental disorders...reported receiving treatment in jail."[11]

The difficulty in achieving a goal of making prisons and jails places where people really can be helped is that it takes courage for governors and state legislators to say that they want to devote more resources to help prison inmates. It's not a popular cause, but a just cause, and one that saves money and lives in the long run.

Tax cuts are much more popular.

Killing by Government: Capital Punishment

The moral leadership of the world is clear on the issue of capital punishment. At the latest count, 106 nations do not have it or do not use it; most of them are democracies. The majority of countries that still retain capital punishment are dictatorships, and we are on the side of dictators, as we are in our opposition to creating the International Criminal Court. Western Europe has abandoned the death penalty. So have Canada and Mexico. Twelve of our own states do not have capital punishment and seven more do not use it, even though it is technically on the books. Turkey, as of this writing, is being denied membership in the European Union for two reasons, one of which is that it retains "the barbaric custom" of capital punishment, a practice it has at least temporarily halted. In an internationally circulated magazine, *Civilization*, we find the following statement: "America's addiction to the ultimate punishment is undercutting its criticism of injustice in other countries.... Throughout Europe, in particular, the death penalty is thought of as simply uncivilized."[12]

Why does the U.S. retain capital punishment? The theory is that it is a deterrent to murder, but any statistical analysis shows that the argument is flawed. Generally the states that do not have the death penalty have a lower rate of murder than the states that do have it. Does that suggest that the death penalty is the cause of murder? No. It simply shows there is no relationship. Do you feel safer in Texas, which accounts for more than one-third of the nation's total executions since 1976—when the Supreme Court reinstated the death penalty—than you do in Iowa, which has the lowest rate of murder in the nation and has not had the death penalty since 1957? Do you feel safer in South Dakota which has a death penalty than you do in North Dakota which does not? South Dakota's slightly higher murder rate than North Dakota's is a matter of statistical interest, simply buttressing the conclusion that it makes no difference.

A 1960 study comparing Michigan and Indiana found an identical rate of murder per 100,000 people (4.3), yet Michigan had higher unemployment, a 40 percent higher minority population and greater population density—all factors that many equate with higher murder rates.[13] The FBI reports that five of the seven states with the lowest murder rate do not have the death penalty. All but two of the twenty-seven states with the highest murder rate have capital punishment. In the Supreme Court case of *Gregg v. Georgia*, Justice Potter Stewart, writing for himself and Justices Lewis Powell and John Paul Stevens, concluded: "Statistical attempts to evaluate the worth of the death penalty as a deterrent to crimes by potential offenders have occasioned a great deal of debate. The results simply have been inconclusive."[14] The reason many favor the death penalty is revenge for horrible crimes. Revenge is not a proper motive for government.

One argument is that the death penalty protects the police force, but again the statistics do not substantiate the argument. The ratio of police deaths are higher, on the average, in states that have the death penalty. A 1920 to 1954 study comparing Rhode Island, without the death penalty, and Massachusetts, which then had it, showed fewer police killings in Rhode Island per 100,000 population.

Innocent people have been, and will continue to be, executed so long as we have the death penalty.

Most citizens are startled to learn that it costs much more to execute someone than to put a person in prison for life. The federal government spent $13.8 million for the defense of Timothy McVeigh, the man who was sentenced to death for bombing the federal courthouse in Oklahoma City. Prosecution costs totaled several million dollars—and personnel and resources had to be diverted from dealing with drug kingpins, serious criminal violations, and other violent crimes.

In an unusual case, Judge Jeffrey Simmons of small and economically depressed Vinton County, Ohio, ruled that the prosecution could not ask for the death penalty because the costs to the county would be too great. He noted: "While the court has authority to approve expenses, it would be disingenuous to suggest that a trial judge can consider such requests without an awareness of the financial impact on this county. The court finds that the potential impact of financial considerations could compromise the defendant's due process rights in a capital murder case."[15]

The discriminatory aspects of capital punishment are repugnant to anyone who believes in equal justice. Those who receive the death penalty are those who cannot afford good lawyers. One recent study concludes: "The death penalty is imposed not for the worst crime, but for the worst lawyer."[16] A series of articles in the *Chicago Tribune* examined 285 cases where the death penalty sentence was imposed between 1977 and 1999, but in most cases not carried out. It was found that 39 of the defendants had attorneys who were later disbarred or disciplined and 46 cases had used "jailhouse snitches" (prisoners who have an incentive for favorable testimony for the prosecution, testimony that frequently is not reliable) as the basis for conviction. In 35 instances African Americans were sentenced to death by juries who were all white. In twenty instances lab work turned out to be faulty, either through fraud or sloppy work. Findings like these caused Illinois Governor George Ryan to courageously suspend the use of the death penalty during his four years in that office, 1999–2002, and in his last days shift 160 people from death row to life in prison.

It is true that on rare occasions, such as Timothy McVeigh's, there are highly visible crimes where adequate counsel is provided the defendant and he still receives the ultimate punishment, but the number of those that occurred in the last century can be counted on one hand. And it is not simply a matter of poverty. It is old-fashioned, crude racism that emerges. For example, this commentary on Florida appears in the *Harvard Law Review:* "The ratio of offenders on death row to arrestees for murder during a felony is 31 percent for murderers of white victims as compared to one percent for murderers of black victims.... Forty-seven percent of the black defendants arrested for murdering a white victim were sent to Florida's death row; only 24 percent of the white defendants arrested for murdering a white victim received the same sentence. When both the victim and offender were black, the ratio sank to one percent. There were no white persons on death row for killing only a black person; there has never been such a person on Florida's death row in living memory."[17] That appeared in 1981, but the pattern in state after state after state remains the same, with statistics obviously varying somewhat. In Illinois in 2002, 67 percent of those housed on death row were people of color, who constitute only 13 percent of the state's population. In Kentucky, more than one thousand African Americans have been murdered since 1975, but as of January 2000, all thirty-nine death row inmates—and all those who have been executed since 1975—are there for killing a white person. One other not-so-minor point: As of 1998, 98 percent of the chief prosecuting attorneys in states with the death penalty were white, one percent were African American.[18]

In July 2000, the European Parliament went on record urging the United States to drop the death penalty. Since 1990 only six nations have executed prisoners for crimes committed when they were less than eighteen years of age: Iran, Nigeria, Pakistan, Saudi Arabia, Yemen—and the United States. The nation that has executed the most: the United States of America.[19] As of August 2002, we had eighty on death row for crimes committed by persons under the age of eighteen.

Even for the most horrendous crimes, what sounds tough may not be wise. Osama bin Laden's distorted thinking that led to the September 11th massacre gave him status among radicals in the Islamic world, but the publicity we gave him in calling for his death elevated his stature in those circles. When people tell me they have ridden in taxis in other nations and seen the picture of Osama bin Laden displayed, I wonder how much we may have caused that misplaced adulation.

Three days after September 11th, my then eleven-year-old granddaughter, Reilly Knop, wrote to the president: "I think you are making a bad choice to just go ahead and kill those responsible for terrorism. In first grade I learned that you should not fight back when you are hit. I think you should have a court case and give the terrorist group a severe punishment, but not kill them. I know that they hurt and destroyed many people's lives, but if we kill them we will have a bigger number of lives and families destroyed. This is my advice." Neither her parents nor I knew anything about the letter until it had been sent.

In the late 1600s, a prominent French woman wrote to her daughter: "You talk very pleasantly about our miseries, but we are no longer so jaded with capital punishments; only one a week now, just to keep up appearances. It is true that hanging now seems to me quite a cooling entertainment."[20] We look back and are aghast at their insensitivity. What do you think the reaction of people will be a century from now as people read about our executions?

Tocqueville, after quoting the above letter, notes progress in dealing with criminal offenses, but adds: "In no country is criminal justice administered with more mildness than in the United States.... The Americans have almost expunged capital punishment from their codes."[21]

How times have changed!

The Law Can Be So Cumbersome That It Is an Impediment to Justice

"Let's pass a law on that" is often the cry when there is an abuse, and frequently a change in the law is needed. Sometimes, however, this is not the wisest course. It is also important to use the law responsibly.

Often the finest defenders of our civil liberties are lawyers. Those who safeguard us from the abuses of government or bad business practices or unethical physicians and offenders in every field are overwhelmingly those who practice law. Attorneys have special responsibilities to uphold the cause of justice and to defend our basic freedoms. Tocqueville commented: "The aristocracy of America is on the bench and at the bar."[22] Today lawyers play a disproportionately large role in determining public policy. One-third to one-half of the U.S. Senate membership, for example, is composed of attorneys; the percentage in the House is slightly smaller. Key staff members are frequently lawyers. Even though it is not required by the Constitution, all current members of the U.S. Supreme Court are lawyers. Attorneys have a duty to be guardians of our civil liberties, and not simply to use the law as a tool to make a good living.

We have more lawyers per hundred thousand people than any other nation. We have far too many lawsuits, and those who can afford to hire the lawyers are too often not those whom the law was intended to protect.

Labor unions who win a contested election for representation of workers often find the law a barrier to representing workers, even when they get a majority vote, because of delaying and costly lawsuits. Businesses sometimes find the law borders on extortion when they are faced with the choice between settling threatened lawsuits or assuming the considerable costs of lengthy litigation. Poor people generally assume that the law will not help them, and too often that assumption is correct.

Alternative methods of resolving minor disputes without going to court are used in several states; this is an important step forward. Someone who buys a defective refrigerator can't ordinarily afford to enter into formal court litigation to get justice.

Having court and legal costs assessed against someone filing a clearly frivolous suit—often as part of a shakedown—is the law in many states and in federal law, but the judges too infrequently use this tool.

We must make sure the law is an assist to justice, not a barrier. It usually is helpful. Martin Luther King Jr. told the *Wall Street Journal:* "It may be true that the law cannot make a man love me, but it can keep him from lynching me, and that's pretty important."[23]

THE CRY TO DEREGULATE has its flaws, as the nation discovered during the California energy crisis of 2001 and business scandals of 2002. Regulation can be a basic protection for our citizens. However, too often through unpublicized appointments, the regulating agency becomes captive to the interests it is to regulate, a problem that is particularly severe in the states. At the federal level too, well-intentioned laws are often badly distorted when regulations are drafted. Legislative oversight of regulators is important in protecting the public.

IN THE FRONTIER STATES early in our history, hard-drinking men often took the law into their own hands, and the innocent often ended up being victims of that action along with the guilty. When an already unpopular Presbyterian minister, Elijah Lovejoy, who edited an anti-slavery newspaper in slave-holding Missouri, denounced the mob action that burned to death a free black tied to a tree, he knew his words would ignite opposition. A federal judge, Luke Lawless—Gilbert and Sullivan could not have picked a better name—found no one in the mob guilty but denounced Lovejoy and his newspaper. Lovejoy's editorials, he said, "fanatasize the negro and excite him against the white man."[24] Judge Lawless read the jurors Lovejoy's printed statement that "Slavery is a sin and ought to be abandoned" and noted that it "seems to be impossible that while such language is used and published...there can be safety in a slaveholding state." He called for action against Lovejoy: "It is all important that the negro population within our bounds should be saved from the corrupting influence to which I have thought it my duty to call your attention...but it will be asked, is there no remedy for this monstrous evil? I am compelled to answer that I know of none."[25]

The combination of his finding no one guilty in the mob and his public exhortation to the grand jury (which met in public in those days) was virtually a call for more mob action, this time against Lovejoy. It came. A parade of people followed a man with a bass drum and threw Lovejoy's equipment into the Mississippi River. Lovejoy moved across the river to Alton, Illinois, technically a free state but one with strong pro-slavery sentiment in its southern half. Lovejoy continued his opposition to slavery and in 1837 a mob killed him. Because of the strong pro-slavery sentiment in the state, Illinois public officials either sided with the mob or were silent. Three months later, however, a twenty-eight-year-old state representative, Abraham Lincoln, gave the first speech that provided an insight into the nation's future leader. He did not mention Lovejoy's name, but everyone knew to whom he was referring when he denounced mob action. His speech included these words:

> Let every man remember that to violate the law is to trample on the blood of his father, and to tear the charter of his own, and his children's liberty. Let reverence for the laws be breathed by every American mother, to the lisping babe that prattles on her lap....In short, let it become the political religion of the nation; and let the old and the young, the rich and the poor, the grave and the gay, of all sexes and tongues, and colors and conditions, sacrifice unceasingly upon its altars.[26]

That is still sound advice.

CHAPTER NINE

HUMILITY

The higher we are placed, the more we should be humble.
—Cicero[1]

Humility is often phony. Feigned humility is easily detected. I remember when a state senator, after making a speech that exceeded good taste in being self-laudatory, was advised by the late Judge George Moran to try to be more humble, that his lack of humility really turned people off. In the next speech the state senator spent a good deal of his time bragging to the audience about how humble he was. And he managed to get reelected, barely.

There are enough flaws in each of us, and in all of us collectively as a nation, that boasting comes across to others as annoying and sometimes arrogant. When pride is too much on display the result is not admiration for our nation, but disdain. We don't need to use Emily Dickinson's line: "I'm nobody, who are you?" However, both individually and collectively, reasonable and genuine modesty is appreciated.

Patriotism involves more than flying a flag or singing a song or posting a sign. I sometimes feel like stopping the cars with flags and asking the occupants if they voted in the last election. When I hear a host on a talk radio show boast, "We're better than other people," I say a silent prayer, hoping that not too many visitors to our country hear that nonsense. Am I proud to be an American? You bet. Does that make me better than someone in Germany or Guatemala or Botswana? Of course not.

A little of the same lack of humility (although usually not crudely put) appeared on a religious basis after September 11th, when speakers would assert inaccurately that the current struggle against terrorism was one between Christianity and Islam, the clear implication being that we (in the Christian world) were right and they were wrong. The not-so-subtle message beneath those words was, "We're good and they're bad."

A generally circulated brochure I mentioned in chapter 2 bears the title: *Why Islam Is a Threat to America and the West*. The authors assert, "Islam is, quite simply, a religion of war."[2] There is much to substantiate that claim—just as there is much that can substantiate the claim that Christianity and Judaism are "religions of war." The Revolutionary War pamphleteer Thomas Paine, like Jefferson a deist (Unitarian in today's terminology), but a critic of traditional religions, wrote: "What is it the Bible teaches us? Rapine, cruelty, murder."[3] There is enough abuse of faith and ideology in all of our religious backgrounds to suggest that humility is in order. When only the negatives of any faith are examined the result is bad—and the result is also a distortion. The we're-good-and they're-bad attitude is based on an unbalanced understanding and leads to violence.

It is common for the president of the United States to state in his State of the Union message to Congress—with about a hundred international ambassadors present—that the United States is the greatest nation in the world. That plays well to the domestic audience.

If others want to say that about us, that's fine. But in the absence of such praise we should not say it about ourselves. Benjamin Franklin, in his famous *Poor Richard's Almanac* with its thoughtful sayings, wrote: "To be humble to superiors is duty, to equals courtesy, to inferiors nobleness."[4] Good advice for everyone! Although in most ways the senior President George Bush showed great sensitivity in international matters, this is from his 1992 State of the Union address: "Americans are the most generous people on Earth.... We are still and ever the freest nation on Earth, the kindest nation on Earth." That is typical of what our leaders too often say, and outside our borders it grates. When the president of the United States speaks, the world listens.

What is no less important for each of us is that when a citizen of the United States speaks, a small part of the world is listening. Novelist Kurt Vonnegut Jr. commented about Hitler and the Holocaust: "Our enemies were so awful, so evil, that we, by contrast, must be remarkably pure. That illusion of purity...has become our curse."[5] It is easy to demonize our opposition, with Hitler obviously being a prime example of someone who personified the worst in humanity. Because our opponents (not just Hitler) are *always* described as evil—and in national emergencies few are willing to stand up and dispute that—by inference then we must be good, we must be virtuous.

It does not follow logically that if the leader of another nation is a ruthless dictator, we should attack that country. We should let the world know that we believe strongly in certain basic human rights, including the right of people to freely choose their leaders and the right to free speech and freedom of religion, but we might add a touch of humility that too often is not mentioned: We recognize that we have substantial imperfections in our own practices. The addition of a little humility strengthens the fundamental message we want to send to oppressed people.

What would you think of a state's chief executive who said, "I'm the greatest governor in the nation!" It comes across as arrogant, even if true. The same holds for a country. At one point the French often boasted, "We live under the most powerful king in the world."[6] No one could deny the truth of what they said, but saying it did not help the French cause. A former deputy secretary of defense in the Reagan and senior Bush administrations in viewing the current world scene expresses concern about "the growing perception of U.S. arrogance held by our friends and allies."[7] As a candidate, George W. Bush advocated practicing humility in dealing with other nations, but that wise course deteriorated badly a few months after September 11th. The temptation to do or say what is popular for the domestic audience overpowers too many administrations and harms our conduct of foreign policy. We would be wise to keep in mind the words of John F. Kennedy in his inaugural address about working with others on international issues: "United, there is little we cannot do; divided, there is little we can do."

One of the nation's thoughtful ambassadors for many years, David Newsom, after his retirement wrote his reflections and noted: "One legacy of past attitudes toward the new nations is a sense that the United States knows best and has little need either to consult or involve those of another country in U.S. decisions."[8] A poll in Canada finds that a majority of our neighbors view us as a bully in international affairs. Polls in other nations show that even more dramatically. We do not solve that image problem—which has an impact on the cooperation we receive from other nations—simply by announcing that we're not a bully. We do it by listening to others, working with others when we can, and toning down language that is too boastful. What is true of individuals is true of nations. Others tend to see our defects more than we see our own. Those defects are much more tolerable if they are not accompanied by arrogance.

We have ample reasons of substance for humility. It also strengthens our nation's effectiveness as a world leader.

CHAPTER TEN

COMPASSION

The quality of mercy is not strained.
It droppeth as the gentle rain from heaven
Upon the place beneath. It is twice blessed:
It blesseth him that gives, and him that takes.
—William Shakespeare, *Merchant of Venice*, 1596

Those who founded our nation set up a structure that differed dramatically from their European roots in giving all citizens rights, in contrast to the formal upper and lower classes in Europe. However, as I have noted, "all citizens" did not include Native Americans, or African Americans, or women—significant deficiencies.

In the fundamental struggle between Alexander Hamilton and Thomas Jefferson, in which Hamilton favored giving a stronger voice to those of wealth who owned property, while Jefferson favored an equal voice for all citizens, Jefferson prevailed—though our present system of financing campaigns is tilting things in Hamilton's direction. Hamilton's idea of property ownership as a prerequisite for voting is repugnant to us today, but most of the state constitutions required it. Jefferson, who was not present at the Constitutional Convention, faced an uphill fight. New York required owning property valued at twenty pounds and Massachusetts required property valued at sixty pounds. Only three states had what we would call free elections: Pennsylvania, New Hampshire, and Delaware. Members of North Carolina's then-called House of Commons (lower house) had to own at least one hundred acres. States had hefty financial requirements for qualifying to become a governor. That the Federal Constitution had no requirement of property or wealth to hold elective office or to become a federal judge meant another step toward equality, a significant move that came only after a struggle.[1] By the time of Andrew Jackson's administration, the states had almost entirely abandoned property qualifications as a requirement for voting or holding office, though remnants of that practice survived into the twentieth century.

Visitors to our nation were impressed by the huge difference between Europe and the United States in equal rights for citizens and by the classless society we appeared to be building. They were particularly impressed because, ironically, it was being built by people like Thomas Jefferson and George Washington and others who at the time were part of the financial and cultural elite.

I don't recall specifically reading the word "compassion" in the writings of Thomas Jefferson, George Washington, John Adams, or James Madison. But their actions moved us toward opportunity for everyone, and included Washington freeing his slaves. "They should have done more," some readers may say, and in hindsight all of us could do much better. A year before the signing of the Declaration of Independence, Abigail Adams wrote to her husband John Adams: "We have too many high sounding words and too few actions that correspond with them."[2] But the words and actions were enough to launch a nation toward equality for all its citizens.

Through those early decades of the nation there too often was brutal treatment of Native Americans and a reluctance to face the evils of slavery. At the same time, citizens engaged in efforts to help people disabled by loss of eyesight or hearing and in providing economic incentives for people of limited means to pioneer in the frontier. Small but active groups were fighting slavery and volunteer associations were working on a variety of social ills. In 1831 there were more than 270,000 members of temperance societies in a hard-drinking national population of less than 13 million. The number of people in these societies was larger than the population of New York City, then 202,000.

During the Great Depression years of the late 1920s and the 1930s we discovered that when we are compassionate, we not only help the impoverished and unemployed, we also help the nation. Sensible generosity, we learned, is not only humanitarian, it also aids all of us who, through our government, are donors. The creation of Social Security was an act of compassion that reduced the percentage of older Americans who live in poverty from 35 percent to 10 percent. But it did more than that. We discovered that, by having provided older Americans with a steady source of income—almost all of it spent rather than saved—we established a floor below which the economy of the nation cannot sink. No longer is there likely to be an economic depression like that of the late 1920s and 1930s, not solely because of Social Security, but because of that and unemployment compensation and other protections for the poor which help all of us. That does not mean that there will be no dips in the economy. Fluctuations will continue, but the wild gyrations are much less likely. If we had created Social Security and some of these programs out of enlightened selfishness, it would have made sense. While motivation on many things is mixed, we basically acted to protect the elderly, and we ended up protecting them and ourselves.

Our response to the less fortunate after World War II embraced those suffering in Western Europe and, to a lesser extent, in the Asian nations involved in the war. A rare combination of courage on the part of President Harry Truman and courage on the part of the Republican leadership that controlled Congress gave the world the Marshall Plan, unpopular at the time in our country, but historians and economists agree that it was one of the wisest—and most generous—actions ever undertaken by any nation. Now we are proud of what was then unpopular.

But the national mood to help those abroad and at home gradually changed. Four major causes account for the shift:

First, as polls came to increasingly dominate politics, those in leadership positions looked more and more to popularity rather than facts or needs or history to make decisions.

Second, as our standard of living rose, we became more and more self-satisfied. If we were doing all right economically, we assumed that others must be doing so also, and if they weren't it was their own fault.

Third, almost unnoticed, we became a nation that was much more segregated on the basis of economics. The concerns of the poor in our nation as well as in other nations became more distant, less real, less pressing. Unless we live in a small town, the people struggling to find food and shelter and health care live "over there" somewhere, and the mile or two miles or ten miles that separate us could just as well be a hundred miles. Rarely does the media—particularly television and radio—remind us of the poor, because it doesn't help ratings.

Fourth, our system of financing political campaigns has made office-holders and candidates much more sensitive to those who are economically fortunate than to those who are impoverished. As I prepare this manuscript, a letter arrives from a former student of mine who attended a "candidate school" and came away deeply disillusioned. "I was amazed to hear advice [to] only listen to the people who give you the most money."[3] I do not suggest this is typical, but I am sure any candidate school will tell those in attendance to pay great attention to large donors. However, the big contributors are not the people who are unemployed or can't pay their hospital bills.

Some would add a fifth reason: More and more of those who occupy high public office are wealthy. I am uneasy about this concern, because among those most sensitive to the problems of the economically disadvantaged during my years in government were wealthy officials like Democrats Senator Edward Kennedy and

Senator Howard Metzenbaum and Republicans like Senator John Danforth and Representative Amo Houghton. I am not sure the conclusion about wealth causing insensitivity is generally true for office-holders; I have seen no study on this. I see new wealthy members, like Senator Jon Corzine of New Jersey, who are compassionate, and not just with words. However, I have also had discussions with wealthy office-holders who obviously do not understand the economic struggle many face. One of the worst was someone who came up the hard way to become a multi-millionaire, whose attitude bore the stamp: "I made it. If they work hard enough they can make it too."

Interestingly, Tocqueville in 1831 expressed concern about not paying public officials adequately. If they do not receive sufficient income, he wrote, "a class of rich and independent public functionaries will be created who will constitute the basis of an aristocracy; and if the people still retain their right of election, the choice can be made only from a certain class of citizens."[4]

WHILE WRITING THIS BOOK I visited one of our state prisons. My purpose was to see a prisoner, Robert Felton Jr., whom I had not met but with whom I had corresponded and who seemed unusually articulate. I also wanted to get some feel for the situation in that prison.

Robert Felton Jr. is in isolation (often called segregation), in part because of a history of minor mental problems that have caused him to behave in a disruptive manner. However, the state Director of Corrections, Donald Snyder, in a report to me said that his conduct has been good for eighteen months—but he remains in segregation. He is permitted out of his seven-by-twelve-foot cell for one hour a day, which he spends in a small, enclosed, walled area, twelve feet wide and twenty-eight feet long, with solid concrete walls thirteen feet high, open at the top. His therapist tells me he is doing well. He talks about reading Winston Churchill and other books that I wish my undergraduate or graduate students were reading. He would like to become a counselor to young people. "I want to be able to study and take my GED [high school equivalency] test," he says, adding, "but they won't let me do it." After meeting with him privately, I asked the four prison officials taking me around if it didn't make sense to let him do that. "Yes," the woman in charge of psychological counseling said quickly. The others made no comment. I turned to the warden and asked why he couldn't do it. "We have a waiting list in all our state prisons to study to take the GED test," he responded. "Those in segregation are at the bottom of the list."

This appalls me. We know that passing such a test makes it less likely that prisoners will return to incarceration. But there is no political mileage for a state legislator or a governor to do anything about it. Simply from the viewpoint of dollars saved on prison costs it makes sense to provide that opportunity. Here is one of many instances where compassionate action would not only serve others, but would also serve all of us in terms of both lower taxes and fewer victims of crime in our communities. Even more important, it would be a way of salvaging lives, both in prison and beyond those walls.

As a result of my talking with this one prisoner, it now appears possible that Illinois will change for the better. I have spoken to key officials about this. If we achieve change, the Public Policy Institute that I head at Southern Illinois University will look at the other states. Gradually we will improve things—probably not as rapidly as I would like—but it will happen.

And how did all this come about? Because of two letters. Because one prisoner, Robert Felton Jr., who had read about my concerns, wrote a letter describing the system and telling me about his situation. And because Lois Hayward, the wife of retired Southern Illinois University faculty member John Hayward, wrote to me about this prison and urged me to visit it.

Two small letters. I have learned in my seventy-four years that major changes come about almost always because of small things, because of volunteers, because of the extra effort of one or more people who believe in a cause and do more than complain to their friends about it.

LOOK AT POVERTY IN ILLINOIS, one of the wealthiest states on a per capita basis, and you see what is happening in the nation. Of our state population of 12.5 million, 11.5 percent live in poverty. From 1990 to 2001 per capita income in Illinois went up 25.5 percent, while poverty remained almost constant, rising slightly. When you take a map of Illinois, plot out on it the percentages of those who did not graduate from high school, and then overlay that with the percentages of those living in poverty, the pattern is virtually identical. If we had another map showing the adult illiteracy rate, which we do not know with precision, I am certain the pattern would be the same.

In 1988 President Ronald Reagan noted in a formal address: "Some years ago the federal government declared war on poverty, and poverty won."[5] Two things are wrong with that statement. First, while President Lyndon Johnson labeled it a "war on poverty," it did not receive the resources or attention or bipartisan support a war would receive. It could more aptly have been called "a battle against poverty." Second, while President Johnson's battle did not eliminate poverty, the percentage of American children living in poverty went from 23 percent to 14 percent in five years, no small achievement.

In 1968 CBS had an hour-long documentary on hunger in the United States. Former senator George McGovern recalls:

> The scene that especially moved me was filmed in a school that required all the students to go to the cafeteria at lunchtime, including those unable to eat because they did-n't have the money to pay for lunch. The federal school lunch program...as recently as 1968 did not provide lunches to the poorest children, who could not pay the modest charge. The cameraman focused on a little boy standing at the rear of the room watching the other chil-

dren eat. "What do you think standing here while your classmates are eating?" asked the TV reporter. Lowering his head and looking at the floor, the boy replied softly, "I'm ashamed." "Why are you ashamed?" the reporter asked. "Because," said the boy, "I ain't got no money."

That night, sitting in my comfortable home in northwest Washington with my wife and children nearby, I, too, was ashamed. It was I, a U.S. senator living in comfort, who should be ashamed that there were hungry people— young and old—in my own beloved country.[6]

A few years ago, officials of Bloomsburg State University in Pennsylvania asked me to speak at the dedication of their new library, and because I have written about Abraham Lincoln, they asked me to compare Lincoln's time and ours. Many differences are obvious: radio, television, computers, automobiles, and on and on. However, one difference intrigued me. In Lincoln's time, the great military and economic power was England. But among the semi-industrial nations, the country with the highest percentage of its population living in miserable slums was England. We look back and ask: How could this powerful and wealthy nation have tolerated that? Today the great military and economic power is the United States. Yet, among the industrial nations, the country with the highest percentage of its children living in poverty is the United States of America. Fifty years from now, one hundred years from now, people are going to look back and ask about us: How could they have tolerated that?

Faith leaders particularly can play an important role in reminding their followers of the *demands*—not the requests—of the scriptures of all the major religions to help the poor. Religion should be more than empty words.

For many years I disliked wakes. When I visited a funeral home to express my sympathy to a family I always felt awkward, not knowing the exact words to say. I felt especially uncomfortable joining the small group of people often gathered there who seemed to be thoroughly enjoying themselves. Then my father died in 1969. He had been a Lutheran minister, and his last parish was a small rural congregation where he semi-retired. If you will forgive my boasting, he had the ability to preach an excellent sermon. At his wake, people with rough hands and equally rough English stood in line to tell me how my father had helped them when they really needed help, sometimes with a small loan, more often with a phone call or visit or help at their home when they were temporarily disabled. Every Thursday morning he volunteered to assist at a nearby residential school for the retarded. As people came through that line to express their sympathy I suddenly realized that the great sermons my father preached were not from the pulpit but with his life. I believe that is true for all of us. Our commitment to religious principles is not judged by what we say but by what we do.

THE GROWING DISPARITY between those of us who are more fortunate and those who are less fortunate is an invisible shift in our economy. It is not explosive now, nor will it be in the immediate future, but it will be explosive eventually if not addressed. The problem is worsening because, as a result of our system of campaign financing, those who are more fortunate play a disproportionate role in writing the tax laws. New York University economist Ed Wolff notes: "The richest one percent received 53 percent of the total gain in marketable wealth over the 1983–1998 period. The next 19 percent received another 39 percent. So...the top one-fifth accounted for 91 percent of the total growth in wealth, while the bottom 80 percent accounted for a mere 9 percent."[7] Temporarily softening the impact of this was the economic growth widely experienced by everyone, including a reduction in unemployment. But what is tolerable or ignored in times of prosperity can become explosive in a major recession.

A readable and well documented book by Kevin Phillips, *Wealth and Democracy*, tells the story of the gradual shift in resources. He notes Congressional Budget Office figures for average household income for 1979 to 1997, showing the lowest one-fifth moving from $9,300 a year in 1979 to $8,700 a year in 1997. For the top 1 percent, after-tax income went from $256,400 to $644,300.[8] Food stamps and earned income tax credit soften those bottom figures, but if these trends continue—and they will increase under the 2001 tax laws—eventually greed will become self-destructive. In 1989 *Business Week*, not a radical journal, commented: "The Great Divide between rich and poor in America has widened and is perhaps the most troubling legacy of the 1980's."[9] In September 2002, the Census Bureau released its report of income for 2001 compared to 2000, showing an increase in poverty families of 1.3 percent, a drop of $934 in average family income, and an increase in income of $1,000 for the top 5 percent.[10] Because of the drop in the stock market, most in the top 5 percent experienced a reduction in net assets greater than the $1,000 gain in income. But the growing spread in income difference is disquieting.

A column in an Israeli publication, critical of the gap between the poorest and wealthiest in that nation, noted: "People can't put food on their table. The divide between the richest and poorest tenths of the population is the widest of any Western nation with the exception of the U.S."[11]

Msgr. Bryan Hehir, the highly respected chief executive officer of Catholic Charities, notes that in the 1990s the U.S. experienced greater growth than anyone could have dreamed, but he adds: "This most miraculous growth did not lift all the boats. The rising tide lifted many, but it left some behind."[12]

What most impressed Tocqueville about this nation was our equality of opportunity. We continue to be better than many nations in this, but a growing insensitivity to the less fortunate in our country and beyond our borders is morally repugnant and eventually will result in a severe legislative backlash that will lack both balance and wisdom. Arthur Sulzberger Jr., former publisher of the *New York Times*, says: "I spent three of the worst educational months of my life at the Harvard Business School back in the early 80's. I would not have worked for the company they wanted me to run. In my judgment, they confused value with wealth."[13] If we so concentrate on adding wealth that we ignore more fundamental values and do not assist those who need help, our wealth will quickly tarnish. Daniel Schorr, the news commentator, recalls a Depression sign in a New York delicatessen: "Eat here or we'll both starve."[14] There is a sign hanging over humanity for all those thoughtful enough to see it: "Share here, or we'll all suffer."

After World War II, under the Marshall Plan, we devoted a higher percentage of our national income (GDP) to helping the poor beyond our borders than any other nation. By the year 2002, with the bipartisan consent of Congress, we had slipped dramatically. Of the twenty-two wealthiest nations, ours had the lowest percentage of our income going to help the world's needs. Spain and Portugal are ahead of us. Norway, Denmark, and the Netherlands each contribute at least seven times more than we do as a percentage of national income. American generosity has shrunk, and we have harmed ourselves. A *Washington Post* writer notes: "While America has enjoyed one of its most prosperous decades ever in the 1990s, it has also set a record for stinginess. For as long as people have kept track, never has the United States given a smaller share of its money to the world's poorest."[15] The need is immense. A news story from the United Nations includes these two paragraphs:

> The picture in sub-Saharan Africa is especially stark. Infant mortality rates have improved in much of the world. But in several African countries, the picture is the opposite: 17 percent of the newborns do not live to the age of 5. Sub-Saharan Africa has 10 percent of the world's population and 90 percent of the AIDS orphans.
>
> Squeezed by foreign debt, many governments have spent less and less on basic social services. Some poor countries, the United Nations report found, spend three to five times as much paying off foreign service debt as they do on basic services.[16]

In 1989 Bill Moyers interviewed Henry Steele Commager, then an eighty-seven-year-old, a history teacher for more than sixty years and the author of scores of books. Moyers described the interview as "the closest we can come to interviewing a Founding Father."[17] Commager said: "We have done far less than we could to save the Third World. If we took one-tenth of our military wasting every year, we could take care of these poverty-stricken and desperate areas. We've done nothing to rebuild Vietnam. We dropped eleven million tons of bombs on Vietnam, three times as much as we dropped on the whole of Europe and Japan in World War II. We've given them no compensation at all. We've suddenly become stingy—no Marshall Plan, no great program to help the backward nations of Africa or the backward nations of South America."[18]

Peter Peterson served as Secretary of Commerce under Richard Nixon and headed a task force on public diplomacy which published a report in 2002. Among the observations of this highly experienced group: "Perceptions of the United States are far from monolithic. But there is little doubt that stereotypes of Americans as arrogant, self-indulgent, hypocritical, inattentive, and unwilling or unable to engage in cross-cultural dialogue are pervasive and deeply rooted." The report also notes our "perceived lack of empathy toward the pain, hardship, and tragic plight of peoples throughout the developing world."[19]

If we had followed our earlier tradition of generosity, would we have been the target of terrorists on September 11th? No one knows the answer with certainty. After that date, Pakistan's president, Pervez Musharraf, showed great courage in siding with the United States in our Afghanistan effort, a decision that unsettled many in Pakistan. Columnist George Will commented on what happened six months later:

Pakistan (per capita income $470) has asked this mighty republic (per capita income $26,503)...to remove the quotas on imports of Pakistani pillows and sheets...and

50 percent increases in pajamas, towels, underwear and some other apparel. But the United States ... flinches from some threats, and one of them is a potential torrent of inexpensive Pakistani pajamas.[20]

Pakistan's request received a frigid response from us. Similar decisions to raise tariffs on Canadian timber as well as on steel from other nations are geared to our domestic politics. I favor assistance and retraining for workers out of jobs because of imports as well as loans to businesses to shift into other areas of production. But we should not start a trade war. The response of other nations to our import restrictions is to limit their import of American products. We end up losing jobs. We add to inflation. Everyone loses. We cannot expect other countries to support our international endeavors if we turn a cold shoulder to their concerns. At the World Economic Forum in New York City four months after September 11th, Secretary of State Colin Powell stated accurately that poverty and desperation provide good soil for the non-poor leaders of terrorism to sow their deadly crops.

Writing more than a year before the September 11th terrorist attack, former ambassador and foreign service leader David Newsom made this prophetic observation:

America and the U.S. political system are not prepared at the beginning of the twenty-first century to make any special effort to improve communication with Third World nations.... In light of the many ways that threats from the Third World may ultimately affect the United States, it is not unreasonable to hope that future circumstances will bring a reorientation of directions. One can only hope it will not be too late.... The United States with its wealth, cannot be effective diplomatically in the rest of the world unless it finds better ways to use portions of that wealth to raise the standards of living in other countries.[21]

That requires maturity on the part of our leaders. A tiny baby cries in church or wherever people may be assembled, totally oblivious to how others may react. That self-centeredness gradually changes as we grow older, as we mature. Some people never mature and their self-absorption eventually can lead to serious physical and mental problems. Mature, healthy people are interested in others.

The same is true of a nation. Self-absorption is understandable, but too much of it is unhealthy. We need enough self-centeredness to take care of ourselves, but we must also be sensitive to and interested in others. That balance is important for a healthy person and a healthy nation.

The Irish entertainer Bono, who has shown a heartening interest in the developing world, spoke at an Africare dinner and said: "[This year] two and a half million Africans are going to die of AIDS. People tell me it's going to take an act of God to stop this plague. I don't believe that. I think God is waiting for us to act.... God is on His knees to us, waiting for us to turn [from] our own indifference."[22]

Former Nebraska senator Bob Kerrey offers an important observation: "One thing I've learned: Unexpected kindness is the most powerful, least costly and most underrated agent of human change. Kindness that catches us by surprise brings out the best in our natures."[23]

Aid to the poor at home and abroad confronts the psychological barrier of occasional and much-talked-about abuses, most of them pure myth, and a perceived lack of a sense of gratitude on the part of the recipients. Some people relate the story of the person in line ahead of them at the grocery store who purchases lobster with her food stamps. I've heard of that person often, but I have never seen this happen, though I have seen bad judgment used by poor people as well as the rich.

The primary reason this nation should help the poor at home and abroad is that it is in our national interest, as well as morally compelling. Generally that assistance is wisely used by people who have no other choice. But we should not expect perfection or overwhelming gratitude from recipients. When critics of the then-unpopular Marshall Plan said the United States would not get credit for doing it, Harry Truman replied, "I'm not doing this for credit. I am doing it because it is right. I am doing it because it's necessary to be done, if we are going to survive."[24] History makes Truman look great, his critics small. Leo Tolstoy, the great Russian novelist, decided to take the proceeds from one of his novels and give them to the poor, much to the chagrin of his wife and eleven children. After he had given the money to the poor in his neighborhood, he learned that many had used the money to drink themselves into a stupor. "How can I act morally?" he asks himself.[25]

We can be unwise in our method of assistance—and sometimes we have been—but that is not the general rule and should not be an excuse for hard hearts. The anecdotes ignore the results. For example, despite the diminished response of the United States since our generous days under the Marshall Plan, other nations are doing much more. The world has moved from 35 percent of its population being hungry in 1972 to 17 percent in 2002. This is still not a good figure, but it is a dramatic improvement, particularly in light of the growth in world population. Unfortunately, it is too easy to find excuses for a cold selfishness. Enlightened selfishness helps others.

Abraham Lincoln said: "I hold that while man exists, it is his duty to improve not only his own condition but to assist in ameliorating that of mankind."[26]

History will note that when we have been sensibly compassionate, we have been wise.

CHAPTER ELEVEN

COURAGE

The strongest, most generous, and proudest of all virtues is courage.
—Montaigne, 1588[1]

Courage without conscience is a wild beast.
—R. G. Ingersoll, 1882[2]

Since my retirement from the Senate, reporters occasionally ask: "If you could add one quality to our government, what would it be?" The answer is simple: courage. It needs to be combined with integrity and compassion and other values, but the courage shown by so many earlier leaders to create and to elevate the status of our nation has diminished. I cannot quantify it any more than I can quantify beauty, but I recognize it when I see it.

Patrick Henry gave us memorable words in his 1775 speech— "Give me liberty or give me death." He later declined becoming a United States senator or secretary of state under George Washington, and he refused to accept the position of chief justice of the U.S. Supreme Court. But his address advocating the establishment of the Virginia militia to defend against the British not only resulted in that happening, it stirred the soon-to-be nation. In that short speech he also said, "The battle, sir, is not to the strong alone, it is to the vigilant, the active, the brave."[3]

No one questions our nation's strength today. People do question our wisdom. They also question our bravery, and they question whether we are willing to sacrifice for a cause nobler than oil. Much of the criticism is unfair, but we cannot improve our image without changing the substance of our conduct.

In 1993, historian Paul Kennedy wrote, "The evidence suggests that the United States will continue to muddle through. ...But the long-term implication of muddling through is slow, steady, relative decline."[4]

Yesterday, as I was writing this, a high school senior from Mt. Vernon, Illinois, Maria Guerrero, had an appointment with me and told me that she wanted to get into the foreign service and contribute something substantial to international relations. She has a dream, and while it well may be modified, this bright, personable young woman *will* contribute in significant ways. I am seventy-four and have dealt with tens of thousands of citizens and their troubles and their aspirations. I have developed a fairly accurate sense of who will drift and who will lead. It has a little to do with ability, but very little. It is tied to vision and courage and hard work and willingness to sacrifice to achieve a noble end. That applies to a nation also. Maria's story is important because her hopes are entwined with the future of our nation and our world. She is willing —even eager—to enter a career that has a slight element of danger, that will be less financially profitable than other positions but that will pay off in self-satisfaction that comes from the knowledge that she is helping people and literally building a better world.

Courage is not simply a quality needed by people "up there" in the White House or in Congress. It is also required of citizens in Makanda, Illinois, in Oregon City, Oregon, and in Tarpon Springs, Florida. It can be the simple step of writing a letter to the editor of the local newspaper to defend the right of someone who takes an unpopular view, or telling a member of the U.S. House or Senate that you are willing to sacrifice a little so that much of the world is not hungry. Courage is not only putting on a uniform and defending our nation's interest, if need be with your life; it is not only becoming a police officer or fire fighter with the risk those jobs entail; it is also doing things that may seem a little socially awkward, like inviting a family of another creed or racial or ethnic group to your home for dinner. Courage is doing more than the comfortable, and we are a nation that has been lulled into comfortableness.

Generally those who founded our nation were people of means who could have drifted, ignored the slight discomforts that British rule imposed, and lived the remainder of their lives in relative ease. But they showed a willingness to make huge sacrifices for the dream of an independent nation with greater self-rule and opportunity than any country that had yet been created.

From the relatively quiet but statesman-like George Washington, to the quiet but scholarly Thomas Jefferson, to the more boisterous and exuberant among the leaders, their dedication and courage gave the fledgling nation a start greater than any of them might have imagined. But it did take courage! As historian David McCullough notes: "To sign your name to the Declaration of Independence was to declare yourself a traitor to the British Crown. If caught by enemy forces, you would almost certainly be hanged."[5] The day of the signing of the Declaration, John Adams wrote to Abigail: "I do not know what will be the outcome of this. We may pay a very high price. But it is certain that posterity will profit from our sacrifice."[6]

British author and lay theologian C. S. Lewis wrote: "Courage is not simply one of the virtues but the form of every virtue at the testing point."[7]

In commenting on Martin Luther King Jr., former UN ambassador and civil rights activist Andrew Young observed: "What gave his speeches and sermons legitimacy was that Dr. King didn't just talk the talk; he walked the walk from Montgomery to Memphis, enduring jails, beatings, abuse, threats, the bombing of his home, and [ultimately] the highest sacrifice a person can make for a righteous cause."[8] Today we applaud members of our armed forces who serve in Afghanistan or other troubled places of our world, but in terms of personally sacrificing anything to bring about a more just and more peaceful world, most Americans now are unwilling to display the simplest kind of courage, unwilling to make the most minimal effort to build a better society. If our leaders asked us to sacrifice and explained the reasons, the American people would respond. In the meantime, it is easier to sit on a sofa and watch television than bestir ourselves to attend a political meeting or a gathering of citizens to address an injustice. We cheered when John F. Kennedy told us in his inauguration address, "Ask not what your country can do for you; ask what you can do for your country." But our cheers for those ringing words sound hollow today, as leaders follow the public opinion polls and ask for little in the way of sacrifice and the public demands little in the way of real leadership.

Throughout our history we have experienced years—even decades—of drift and unremarkable leadership from time to time, but then leaders arose in the presidency and in the House and Senate or among our citizenry who lifted our vision once again.

In the previous chapter, I discussed the remarkable and generous Marshall Plan we enacted after World War II to help other nations. Shortly before that in 1944, over the objections of all of the veterans' organizations except the American Legion, Congress passed what became known as the GI Bill, a massive educational opportunity program for veterans that immeasurably lifted this nation economically and culturally. But it did not have the popular support of a cash bonus alternative that the other veterans' organizations wanted. The GI Bill, the now-lauded step forward in education, passed in the House-Senate conference committee—after twelve hours of appearing to be dead—by one vote.

Two decades later, and also after great difficulty, the then-unpopular Civil Rights Act of 1964 brought about a bloodless revolution, eliminating the crudest forms of racial segregation that had retarded the nation economically and restricted opportunity for many citizens.

Other milestones in our history could be cited. No significant action ever came about without courage and sacrifice.

What are our dreams today?

There is no end of dreams from which to choose: a Marshall Plan for sub-Sahara Africa, health care coverage for all Americans, something similar to the GI Bill for all college students, a paid semester abroad for all college students who maintain a "B" average during their first two years of college here, a WPA-type guaranteed job opportunity for all Americans that would enrich the nation and substitute for much of welfare. These are among the ideas we should consider. There are many others.

Talk to political leaders and most of them will privately admit that any of these would be great for the nation. However, these leaders are also aware that such steps require sacrifice on the part of the American public and pose the risk of unpopularity for the proponent. If I want to get more education, that requires sacrifice. If I want to improve my country, that requires sacrifice. Polls suggest that sacrifice is not popular, not a good way to get reelected. Perhaps a necessary patriotic sacrifice is not getting reelected, or at least risking that possibility.

One of the observations of those who look at our nation from abroad is that we are no longer willing to take risks for noble causes. They do not question for a moment that we have the most technically proficient defense forces in the world. What they do question is whether we are willing to use those forces in constructive ways when the community of nations determines a need—and it requires sacrifice on our part. They do not question our technology; they question our courage. These critics quietly ignore what we did in Somalia, almost solely for the simple cause of helping starving people, but they do note that when UN troops are needed in Angola, we applaud their use—but don't send any Americans there. When UN troops are needed in Cambodia we praise the idea, but don't risk any American lives. It is a little like the Civil War when draftees in the North could pay to have someone else take their place, an indication of wealth but not of courage.

In 1994, in Rwanda in central Africa, massive, organized, genocidal murder started to take place. As noted earlier, Canadian General Romeo Dallaire, in charge of a small contingent of less than five hundred UN troops, pleaded with the U.S. and Western Europe for five to eight thousand troops to stop the indescribable mayhem. The U.S. quietly led the opposition to doing anything and eight hundred thousand to a million people were slaughtered. When two U.S. senators pleaded for action, the Clinton White House responded that there was no base of public support for doing anything in Africa, a statement containing some truth but a tragically anemic response. The president could have gone on national television and told the American public what we were doing and why and the American people would have supported our joining other nations in stopping the mass murder of men, women, and children.

On the other hand, sometimes it requires courage not to use troops, to resist doing the "macho" thing. Abraham Lincoln's opposition to the war with Mexico in his one term in the U.S. House took courage. Before the latest war in Iraq, public opinion polls showed that 72 percent of the American people wanted an invasion of Iraq. Opposing it in Congress was not politically prudent; it took courage. My guess is that history will be kinder to those political leaders who opposed launching an attack. But whichever side an official takes on this or other issues, it should be on the basis of what is right, not on the basis of political prudence. Real leadership requires courage.

What if President George W. Bush had asked for something less popular than a $1.35 trillion ten-year tax cut which Congress passed? The United Nations reports that ninety-five hundred children a day die because of poor quality water. These are easily preventable deaths. What if $2 billion a year for ten years of that $1.35 trillion were spent to save those children? That would reduce the total tax cut to $1.33 trillion—mostly for the wealthy who are big campaign contributors—and would create a dramatically different image for the United States abroad. Would it have been as popular at home? Perhaps not. But would it have been a more responsible action by the president and Congress? By a huge margin.

Isolating Cuba after Fidel Castro's takeover had immediate popularity, but when that popularity faded—and after it had became apparent that our policy was flawed—we continued the economic isolation of Cuba by the U.S. (and by no other nation) to satisfy a small but vocal group of wealthy, campaign-contributing Cuban ex-patriots in Florida, a key electoral state.

Whether the foreign policy issue is Africa or the Middle East or Cuba or elsewhere, domestic politics too often dictate our response and that is transparent to those outside our borders. They see fat, rich, comfortable Uncle Sam too self-satisfied to risk much politically to build a better world. The children and grandchildren of the heroes of World War II and the sons and daughters of a generous nation that gave the world the Marshall Plan have significantly increased our income and significantly decreased our help to the world's impoverished. We no longer have wrinkles in our bellies. In his first speech to Congress after having the presidency suddenly thrust upon him by the death of President Franklin Roosevelt, Harry Truman told Congress and the nation: "The responsibility of a great state is to serve and not to dominate the world."[9] His sensitivity to other nations resulted in the Marshall Plan, which, like most generous acts, has repaid this country many times over financially and in good will. But it took courage. Unilateralism, the cousin of isolationism, follows the path of isolationism: Go it alone. That plays well to a domestic audience, but it is not what the nation or the world needs.

Yes, September 11th startled us temporarily, but we are not so slowly moving back to taking our siesta from the world's problems. Presidential leadership that displays backbone, legislators who are willing to sacrifice, citizens who demand more than satisfying their own economic appetites—these qualities require courage.

The alternative, as historian Paul Kennedy says, is muddling through and gradual national decline.

The polls will lead us in that downhill direction.

Courage can lead us in a much better direction, one that is in tune with the best of our nation's history and traditional values.

CHAPTER TWELVE

PROTECTION OF OUR EARTH

We are nothing but what we derive from the air we breathe, the climate we inhabit, the government we obey, the system of religion we profess, and the nature of our employment.

—St. John De Crevecoeur, 1782[1]

W e have come from being a nation with few obvious environmental needs and limited public concerns to one that has created a vast national park system and is gradually becoming more aware that the earth is a fragile place and we must do a better job of protecting it.

In 1626—150 years before the Declaration of Independence—the members of the Plymouth Colony in Massachusetts adopted an ordinance that limited the cutting and selling of timber. Fifty-five years later, William Penn ordered that for every five acres of timber land harvested, one acre should be left untouched. Similar small steps, almost unnoticed, occurred around the nation.

However, in a country with a limited population and huge expanses of land, we assumed that nature would renew itself and the scars we imposed on animal and plant life would be temporary. Slowly we learned that this assumption had flaws. At one point we had as many as sixty million American bison (or plains buffalo) roaming our wildernesses, providing food for Native Americans.

But when men and women of European origin moved into those areas with their guns, the number of buffalo rapidly declined, almost to the point of extinction. Most were killed for the sport of it, not for their meat or hides. Today they thrive in small numbers on ranches and farms, providing limited quantities of low-cholesterol meat.

Discordant notes are part of our heritage and, it is to be hoped, will be less a part of our future. In 1933, Luther Standing Bear, a Lakota Indian, wrote:

The Indian was a natural conservationist.... When the buffalo roamed the plains in multitudes he slaughtered only what he could eat and these he used to the hair and bones. One day a buffalo floated by and it was hauled ashore. The animal proved to have been freshly killed and in good condition, a welcome occurrence at the time since the meat supply was getting low. Soon another came floating downstream, and it was no more than to shore when others came into view. Everybody was busy saving meat and hides, but in a short while the buffalo were so thick on the water that they were allowed to float away.... I relate the instance as a boyhood memory. I know of no species of plant, bird, or animal that were exterminated until the coming of the white man.[2]

Tocqueville caught our early assumptions: "The country is boundless and its resources inexhaustible."[3] That attitude gradually changed, but a residue of that outlook remains, and it is a barrier to taking actions that can prevent the deterioration of our natural resources.

The first national park in the world, Yellowstone National Park in Wyoming, became a reality in 1872 when President Ulysses Grant signed the legislation creating it. It launched us into a growing sensitivity about preserving the riches of our environment. Today we are second to Australia in the number of national parks we have. In 1898 Cornell University offered the first class in forestry for college credit. Ten years later President Theodore Roosevelt called the nation's governors together to begin conservation planning. He became the great conservation president. Gradually we started paying more attention to the air we breathe and the water we drink, and we became aware that pollution of our air and water does not have to come automatically with industrial and agricultural progress. In 1906 Theodore Roosevelt signed into law the Pure Food and Drug and Meat Inspection acts, bringing into question for the first time the environmental consequences of animal feed and fertilizers.

As the nation's population grew, we became increasingly aware of the damage people can do to the environment and the constructive things that can happen when we safeguard our rivers and streams and air and soil. Building new homes is good, but what about the trees they displace? We are paying more attention to these basics. After discovering the Caribbean islands, Christopher Columbus wrote to the comptroller of the treasury for King Ferdinand and Queen Isabella of Spain about the "fine harbours, excelling any in Christendom.... [The mountains] are ... covered with a vast variety of lofty trees.... The nightingale and a thousand other sorts of birds were singing in the month of November wherever I went." He goes into detail on trees and flowers and suddenly makes this statement: "To these may be added slaves, as numerous as may be wished for." Then he continues: "Besides I have as I think discovered rhubarb and cinnamon."[4] The jarring sentence about slaves is dropped right into his description of the natural beauty.

The modern environmental movement—or at least much greater environmental awareness—burst onto the national scene with the publication in 1962 of a book by a marine biologist, Rachel Carson, titled *Silent Spring*. Writing primarily about pesticides, she evoked a renewed interest in all aspects of the earth's fragile na-

141

ture. As noted by the editors of a key environmental text, "The publication of [*Silent Spring*] marked the beginning of popular concern about pollution and served as the starting point for the environmental movement."[5]

That movement, like any step forward, has been embroiled in controversy from its infancy. Part of the controversy has been generated because those directly affected by new requirements do not want to change their ways. The status quo is always comfortable for any business or profession or occupation. Some of the confrontation is because people on both sides shout at each other rather than sitting down to listen to each other's goals. I have been modestly successful in getting two sides to these disputes to sit down and—somewhat to their surprise—find they are in accord on major points of apparent disagreement. Part of the controversy comes from the reality that the environmental movement, like every endeavor, is composed of human beings who sometimes make mistakes of judgment in their appropriate passion to save our planet.

During my years as lieutenant governor, the newly created Illinois Environmental Protection Agency (EPA) proposed regulations that would have had the practical effect of requiring cattle and hogs in Illinois to wear diapers—not a policy farmers welcomed. Well intentioned people who didn't know anything about farming drafted the regulations. I called a meeting of the director of the EPA and a few farm leaders. The farmers appeared in my office, but no EPA director. A few minutes after the meeting was scheduled to start he called and said that the agency had made a mistake. The mini-crisis had passed.

Generally I find leaders in the environmental movement careful and reasonable in their approach to problems. In the process, they make this nation a better place for my four grandchildren.

Environmental concerns require more than monitoring the air and water quality and testing the soil. A single mother with three children who lives in an urban public housing project in a high crime area and is afraid to let her children play in the yard outside faces a real environmental problem. Whatever is harmful to life,

142

whether plant or animal, is something that should concern us. Desert Storm, the military response to Iraq's invasion of Kuwait, was a huge—if temporary—military success. But little noticed in our media, it created approximately one million refugees. They can tell you that war is an environmental hazard.

We are in love with cars. I live in a rural area in Illinois and a car is almost essential. But the combination of our love of cars and the lobbying of highway contractors and the automobile industry have prevented us from having the kind of mass transit and railroad passenger service we should have. That would require a subsidy—as every other form of transportation has—on the part of those of us who drive cars. But a six-cent increase in the gasoline tax, one-third going to Amtrak, one-third to urban transit systems, and one-third to rural roads and bridges, while giving a little to the road lobby, would permit significant improvement in rail passenger service. A one-cent gasoline tax brings in $1.2 billion, so two cents for Amtrak would mean $2.4 billion. We are still operating under the illusion that Amtrak and other mass transit operations can pay for themselves. With few exceptions, these services don't pay for themselves anywhere in the world. If in addition to improved service, we could subsidize the cost sufficiently so that urban systems could reduce fares, there is at least the strong possibility that we would relieve automobile congestion and improve air quality—and make better use of our time.

Time magazine asks: "Why can't the U.S. have speedy trains like Europe and Japan?"[6] The answer is that we can, but it will take an investment. If Germany, France, Spain, Sweden, Japan and other nations have high-speed trains, we can too. A decade ago I successfully sponsored legislation in the Senate that required the Department of Transportation to designate five high-speed rail corridors in the nation. That designation took place—slowly. We are inching ahead, but moving toward high-speed passenger service is not a high-speed operation or a high priority for the Department of Transportation. More than fifty million people a year use Amtrak, and still more use other urban mass transit systems.

Many more could and would if we improved services. This is not simply a transportation issue. It is also an environmental concern.

OUR COURSE HAS BEEN one of "two steps forward and one step backward." The U.S. created the Clean Air Act and the Clean Water Act, but in 2002 arbitrarily and unilaterally revoked the Anti-Ballistic Missile Treaty we had signed with the Soviets, opening the door to the possibility of a renewed arms race in the future with devastating consequences to the environment. Twenty years after our nation signed the United Nations Convention on the Law of the Sea, which the U.S. helped develop, the Senate has yet to ratify it.

· Our four percent of the world's population produces roughly one-fifth of the world's air and water pollution. In 1970 the nation had 50 million cars. Thirty years later we had 350 million cars— and more air pollution despite moving to no-lead gasoline. In some ways we are world leaders in environmental sensitivity. Much of the technology developed to enhance the air and water and soil comes from the United States. However, after great speeches in Japan about the environment and global warming, the U.S. backed off of approving the accords developed at the international meeting in Kyoto, much to the chagrin of our friends around the world. We claim it might harm our economy.

It is true that there would be small adjustments, just as every other step forward to protect our environment has called for small sacrifices, but we have both lived with these adjustments and prospered from them. When no-lead gasoline first entered the national debate, U.S. car manufacturers assured us it would devastate the industry, since the standards were impossible to meet and no-lead gasoline really wouldn't do much good. We heard the same about seatbelts! We now have no-lead gasoline and the much-maligned seatbelts are saving thousands of lives each year. In 2002 U.S. car manufacturers reluctantly started developing electric cars and hybrid gasoline-electric cars, which the Japanese are successfully manufacturing and selling in the United States without a federal mandate. That hybrid car reduces pollution from gasoline more than 75 percent. Our manufacturers are now moving slowly in that direction. U.S. car-makers will have to move aggressively to improve the environment voluntarily or be forced by the market and/or by the government to make progress. In the same way, while proposals for using solar and wind energy originally met with strong resistance from "practical" business leaders, there is now a clear thrust in that direction, with leadership being provided by one company headed by a former president of General Motors. I observe solar energy used much more outside the United States than within our borders, but it is coming—and not slowly.

Most nations have signed an agreement to ban the manufacture, sale, and use of land mines, which are harmful to human beings as well as animal life. The United States won't sign the agreement, using as an excuse the explanation that land mines protect South Korea from an invasion by North Korea. Senator Frank Murkowski (R-Alaska)—now governor of that state—and I flew on the first U.S. plane to land in North Korea after the Korean War and had a brief glimpse of that backward nation. A host of things besides land mines prevent them from invading South Korea! I wish those who have made the decision against signing the land mine protocol could join me in visiting Angola in Africa, one of the nations with the most land mines. Many of those devices were manufactured and financed by the United States as we—unwisely—aided one side in that country's civil war. Near the capital city, the Swedish Red Cross has established a center that provides artificial limbs for children who have lost legs or arms to land mines. A five-minute visit to that center would change the mind of the most hard-hearted policymaker who is pandering to our manufacturers. U.S. military leaders with whom I have spoken favor approving the ban.

Our environmental values have been good and bad. We have pioneered in constructive ways, but we have also abused our earth and been reluctant to join other nations in improving this fragile planet.

The need is to do the noble, the good, to take actions that will make this tough but destructible place called earth a safe and healthy place for future generations.

That will require greater cooperation with other nations. Air and water pollution do not recognize national boundaries. Poorer nations cannot be expected overnight to meet the standards that industrial nations set for themselves. The Kyoto agreement on earth-warming gives developing nations more time to meet the standards we have—and it should. Cairo, Egypt, has visibly weaker air pollution requirements than the U.S. has, but the Egyptian per capita income level makes it impossible for that nation to meet rigid standards overnight. Two reports say that Beijing's air is "sixteen times dirtier than in New York and . . . thirty-five times more contaminated than in London."[7] Should they take steps to do something about this? Yes. Their dirty air ultimately hurts us. Can we expect them to move as fast as we could on such problems? No. Our industrialization took place over a century during which pollution went unchecked. Theirs is taking only a few decades as they struggle to join the modern world.

Common sense and sensitivity in working with other nations not only will not harm us but will create a better world for our grandchildren.

CHAPTER THIRTEEN

INTEGRITY

Integrity without knowledge is weak and useless, and knowledge without integrity is dangerous and dreadful.

—Samuel Johnson, 1759[1]

When an organization called Transparency International does its periodic assessment of corruption in various nations, the United States ranks in the top one-fourth with "the good guys." That is encouraging, but the ranking also shows we have work to do, as any close observer of the U.S. political and business scene knows.

The organization's 2002 assessment places Finland at the top of the integrity list, with the United States ranked sixteenth. Among those ahead of us after Finland are Denmark, in second place, and then New Zealand, Iceland, Singapore, and Sweden. Ranked most corrupt was Bangladesh, in close company with Nigeria, Paraguay, Madagascar, Angola, Kenya, and Indonesia.

In any group of human beings, there will be a few who go astray. We have been fortunate in having leaders like George Washington, Thomas Jefferson, John Adams, and James Madison, whose integrity was of the highest order. Yes, we did have in that early crowd an Aaron Burr, who killed Alexander Hamilton in a duel and who was accurately viewed by George Washington as corrupt. Burr served as vice president and later faced a trial for treason. Though the court acquitted him, public opinion then, and history today, are not kind to him. But most of our early leaders had loftier ideas and ideals.

Through the years, blatant corruption marked the activity of many big city political machines, such as Tammany Hall in New York City and its counterparts around the nation. State legislative bodies were bought and sold by the railroads as they have been—and still are—bought and sold by legalized gambling interests in more recent years.

States varied in corruption, depending largely upon the leadership that emerged. Wisconsin had serious bribery problems until the emergence of Robert LaFollette, a strong governor who produced pioneering legislation that much of the nation later adopted. LaFollette also created an atmosphere that made old-fashioned corruption intolerable. Nearby Iowa had a clean reputation, but in Illinois and Indiana bribing legislators, mayors, and governors was common, and many of these people eventually ended up in jail. In 1964, during my years in the Illinois state legislature, I wrote an article (co-authored by journalist Al Balk) for *Harper's* titled, "The Illinois Legislature: A Study in Corruption." I told bluntly what I knew. I said that one-third (a conservative estimate) of the legislators were taking bribes, a practice that few attempted to hide. Some corruption had a thin veneer of legality, such as when legislators who voted for a race track then bought stock in it at ten cents a share that paid one dollar in dividends the first year. The article did not increase my popularity in the state legislature. I thought at the time that would be the end of my political career.

At the federal level our standards were also loose. When Daniel Webster served in the United States Senate, he wrote to the banks saying that if they did not pay his legal fee, he would not introduce their legislation. Today he would be removed from the Senate for doing that.

In 1980, we had the Abscam scandal in which the FBI secretly recorded videos of several federal legislators taking bribes and stuffing $100-bills in their pockets. Those legislators went to prison.

Such blatant corruption is rare on the Washington scene and much less common than it once was in state legislative bodies like that of Illinois. Having served on both the state and national level, I believe I have developed the ability to "smell" corruption. Occasionally I still smell it, but not often.

What has replaced the crude bribery is a more sophisticated and legal form of corruption through our system of financing campaigns. It badly distorts our democracy. It causes moneyed interests to take precedence over the ignored needs of citizens with genuine problems. Investing in the stock market retains great uncertainty (as this is being written), but investing heavily in campaigns for probable winning candidates for key public offices has a big and much more certain financial payoff. It caused Congress to mandate purchasing weapons the Pentagon does not want, such as the B-2 bomber at a cost of $1.4 billion each. It has produced a tax code riddled with special preferences for big campaign donors. It has resulted in questionable appointments to key state and federal posts, appointments in which all too often those who are supposed to be regulated have determined who the regulators are.

The passage in 2002 of the reform bill sponsored by Senator John McCain (R-Arizona) and Senator Russ Feingold (D-Wisconsin) is a small step away from the most blatant abuses. The courage of Senator McCain in hitting this issue hard as he unsuccessfully pursued the Republican nomination for president caused the public to show concern. We also owe thanks to the Enron scandal, which showed how one corporation used campaign cash to work its will.

The successful candidacy of Michael Bloomberg for mayor of New York City is one small indication of the power of money. It was a race in which he spent more money—$70 million—than the entire British nation did in its last national election. Bloomberg, at least, did not end up beholden to interests who wanted him to manipulate policy for their financial advantage. But having to be a

149

multimillionaire to avoid that kind of baggage is not the way the system should work.

INTEGRITY INVOLVES more than not stealing money.

No money changed hands in 1838 when Congressman Jonathan Cilley of Maine killed Congressman William Graves of Kentucky in a duel. It was a dishonorable act perpetrated in the name of honor. Just as violence can emerge from a tortured use of religion, so a deadly duel can emerge from a twisted mixture of pride and integrity. Martin and Susan Tolchin outlined a series of ethical breeches in the history of Congress in an excellent book, *Glass Houses.* They also point out that our ethical standards have gradually risen, contrary to the public image, but serious problems do remain.

It is hard to imagine George Washington or John Adams twisting the truth in order to get votes. All candidates emphasize their points of agreement with local or national public opinion— fair enough as long as they are not deceptive. No candidate stresses his or her unpopular views, but when questioned by reporters or citizens, if deception substitutes for truth, public trust in that candidate and/or public officeholder diminishes. When an office-holder—who frequently also is a candidate—takes an unpopular stand, it is in the office-holder's as well as the public's interest that he or she "go back home" and explain in town meetings and radio call-in shows and other ways why an action serves the public's long-term interest even though it is temporarily unpopular. Lincoln stressed different things in southern Illinois than in northern Illinois in his debates with Stephen A. Douglas in 1858. During the Civil War, Lincoln initially stressed saving the Union rather than the less popular issue of abolishing slavery, but few were unaware of his strong anti-slavery views.

When, under the new constitutional procedure, President Richard Nixon nominated Gerald Ford for vice president after Spiro Agnew's resignation, Ford testified at Senate confirmation hearings. In describing his relations with other members of Congress, he said: "I have never misled them when they might have wanted to hear something gentler than the truth. Truth is the glue that holds government together, and not only government but civilization itself."[2] The confidence that members of Congress and the public had in Gerald Ford came at a time when the nation needed to be healed and have its trust in government reinstated. His was no small contribution.

Candidates and office-holders owe the public the truth, and they ought to live by their convictions.

To go against what you believe as an office-holder or candidate in order to curry votes and use the lame excuse, "I'm doing what the people want" is to fail to understand how Madison and Jefferson and others envisioned the way in which our nation would operate, and it fails to pass the test of integrity. It adds to public cynicism about politics. "You can't believe anything they say," is a widely held belief about candidates and office-holders. The reality is better than the public image, but the reality is far from what it should be. Pandering to the latest public opinion polls too often is a substitute for truthfulness.

There is another less visible danger in this approach to politics. Once a candidate or office-holder has taken a popular stand that he or she believes is wrong, after repeating the position a few times and finding straws to buttress the argument, that person starts to believe his or her own statements. Philosopher Hannah Arendt said: "Deception without self-deception is well-nigh impossible."[3] When you try to fool the public, you also end up fooling yourself.

OUR GOVERNMENT ALSO REFLECTS our culture. If the person who repairs your furnace is dishonest, and the customer at a grocery store does a little shoplifting, and the college student cheats on an exam or a paper, don't be surprised if the person who represents all these people in government also lacks integrity. Honesty doesn't just come from the top down; it is built from the base up.

When people in the media criticize office-holders for simply pandering to public opinion rather than doing what is right, that criticism too often rings true. But when the same media people tell us they cut back on international news coverage because it hurts their ratings, it makes their political criticisms ring hollow. Studies show that TV violence that glorifies the mayhem on entertainment shows does harm to children and to some adults, but it makes money. One of the great historical writers of recent decades, Barbara Tuchman, observed: "The [media] will accept as great almost anything that they think is funny or that they think will sell . . . that appeals to the mass public, even if it's basically trashy."[4]

Yes, integrity must be exercised by all of us. And those in the media who have such a pervasive impact on our lives have a special responsibility to give us the opportunity to become well informed.

CLOSELY ALIGNED WITH INTEGRITY is loyalty. But loyalties can shift, and occasionally integrity may require what appears to be disloyalty. Should someone be loyal to a political associate who has become corrupt, or loyal to the principle of honest government? Integrity clearly demands the latter.

We want to be loyal Americans, loyal to a nation that had its birth in disloyalty. Were they wrong to be disloyal to England? Immigrants to our country break their allegiance to Germany or Italy or India or Nigeria when they come here. They take a loyalty oath to our country. Does that make them disloyal to their mother country?

We want our citizens to be loyal to the law, but Martin Luther King Jr. and hundreds of civil rights activists purposely violated the laws of segregation and brought about a much-needed bloodless revolution in our nation. Were they wrong to do that?

In Germany, men (and a few women) who pledged obedience to the laws carried out the orders of Hitler and his henchmen and massacred six million Jews. They were, in a sense, loyal.

In Israel, some of those serving in the Israeli military reserves refuse to participate in the occupation of Palestinian territory. Are they disloyal?

In each serious armed conflict in which the United States has been engaged we have had a military draft. But Quakers (Friends) and others are conscientious objectors and have refused to serve. Were they being disloyal?

From the earliest days of our nation there has been a recognition that we should be proud of our nation and of our state or city or school or family, but there are limits to loyalty.

Sometimes loyalty requires that we do unpopular things. It demands more than flag-waving. It may require defending the right of someone to speak on behalf of policies that you abhor, an act of much greater loyalty than flying a flag from your car. It may mean standing up for the right of a black or Latino family to move into a white neighborhood. It may require something as simple—or not so simple—as discouraging parents at a Little League game from shouting obscenities at a player or umpire or other parents.

Loyalty—like patriotism—implies a sense of civic responsibility, not simply mouthing high-sounding phrases. Loyalty is directed not simply to a collective entity of 280 million people we call our country. It is loyalty to our values, to a sense of community, whether in our home or religious institution or civic club or athletic team or some other entity.

There is also a growing sense that humanity is not divisible; that while we are proud to be Americans, we have a common bond with all people; that in addition to being loyal American citizens, we also should be loyal world citizens. To the extent such sensitivity is nurtured, it is less likely that our children will be involved in violent conflicts or become victims of terrorist attacks.

Loyalties should have limits. There is a moral law higher than any ordinance passed by your city council or state legislature or by Congress, higher than getting into a fight with a Chicago Cubs fan if you are a St. Louis Cardinal supporter. If leaders of one religious faith ask us to respond to adherents of another belief with violence, or even with words of hatred, most of us sense that is a distortion of religion that reflects unfavorably on us.

Human institutions have flaws. Loyalty demands support when they are right, and loyalty sometimes demands opposition.

After September 11th the nation experienced a healthy coming together at everything from baseball and football games to religious services. Flags appeared everywhere. We sang the national anthem and "God Bless America" and the first stanza to "America the Beautiful." But sometimes we forget these words in the second stanza:

> America! America!
> God mend thine every flaw,
> Confirm thy soul in self-control,
> Thy liberty in law!

CHAPTER FOURTEEN

AND ...

We don't live fully enough or aim high enough.
—John M. Buchanan, 2003[1]

Professed noble values have almost no meaning unless people put legs on those ideas, unless citizens strive to make them a reality. That has always been true, but its importance is magnified with the startling and tragic development of the terrorist attack of September 11th. That awakening call is becoming fainter. As the *New York Times* editorialized a year later, "The mood of sacrifice is fading, the window of opportunity for [harnessing] the patriotism generated by September 11 slowly closing."[2] For those sensitive to the needs of our society and our world, this makes the demand for us to act even more compelling.

Americans have a rich heritage for which we should be grateful. Political observer Mark Shields writes: "Each of us has been warmed by fires we did not build, each of us has drunk from wells we did not dig. We can do no less for those who come."[3]

To live in a nation where we can speak our minds freely and worship as we wish, where we can select our leaders and run for public office if we desire is no small blessing. In addition, Americans have one of the highest standards of living in any nation, though many of our citizens do not share fully in this benefit.

Historian Barbara Tuchman told Bill Moyers in an interview that heroes have "a nobility of purpose."[4] What is *our* nobility of purpose? What is our dream for this nation? What are we doing to lift our vision? What are we doing to make our dreams—our vision—become a reality?

HERE ARE A FEW practical suggestions.

Focus on one or, at most, two issues that you believe could ennoble your community, your state, or our nation. You cannot be effective working on twenty-six ideas, or even ten. Over time that may become possible for you, but start with a narrow focus. What do you believe *strongly* would improve things? If you are strong in your beliefs, you are more likely to succeed, because small barriers will not stop you.

Read newspapers and magazines to find out more about the first issue you have chosen. Check it out on the Internet. Go to your local library to get books on the subject. Find out what the opponents to your idea say—and remember that every genuinely good idea generates opposition. Don't study things indefinitely, but gather enough substance on the question so that you feel comfortable talking about it and have the ability to answer questions that others might pose.

Once you have one or two subjects picked out, pull together six or eight of your creative friends in your home or in someone else's home to brainstorm. Do it in a home rather than a restaurant, where you will have interruptions. Give everyone a pen and paper so they can make notes as the evening progresses. You should come up with roughly twenty ways of achieving your goal, or perhaps you might shift your goal. There will be at least two or three solid ideas resulting from your discussion.

That evening, or maybe in a subsequent meeting, talk about what you can do to *really* get something done. Come up with concrete plans. Early in the stages of working on this subject, make sure to keep your immediate goal easily achievable. After you take the first tentative step—like a young child—gradually you will become more effective and you can take larger strides. For example, if you believe we should do more to assist hungry people beyond our borders, get those friends together and plan how you will generate thirty letters to your House and Senate members in Washington. That appears easy, but you will discover that although half the people who pledge to write letters have good intentions, they won't actually do it. Your letters will probably be the only ones those legislators receive on that subject during the month.

Then follow through. Make sure the goal you've proposed in your letters is achieved. If you saw someone struggling to survive in a swimming pool, you would jump in to save that person's life. I have said many times that each letter generated on behalf of helping the desperately poor around the world literally saves a life. It is not as direct as jumping into a pool, but just as effective. If a tiny fraction of one percent of our population did this, we would be devoting much more than one-half of one percent of our federal budget to assist the world's impoverished. Whether this is your issue or something else is, keep following through. That is important in tennis and baseball—and in public policy. Once you have achieved this first important step—and it is important—you are ready to take additional steps.

What you recommend depends on your goals. If you want to get foreign language education in your local grade schools, you will go about it differently than if you want to get more educational services for men and women in prison or if you want to push legislators to look at the long-range need for water in many desperate areas of the world.

After making that first move, here are additional steps you may want to consider:

- Send a letter to the editor of your local newspaper, and get two or three others in your group to do the same. Such letters are well read, both by the public and by officeholders.

157

- Contact your local civic groups and offer to do a program for them. They are almost always looking for people to make presentations at their meetings.

- Do the same for an organization within the local religious branches in your community. When you speak to them (or to the civic groups), suggest something concrete they can do as individuals.

- Offer a $100 or $200 prize to the high school senior in your area who writes the best essay on the subject. It not only calls attention to the issue but also generates interest on the part of all who write the essays—and their parents.

- If you have enough resources, make it a $1,000 prize and offer it to students at the nearest college or university.

These are all "little things," but they are the things that will gradually shift history constructively or destructively.

DON'T FORGET TO DREAM. I suggest that the first steps be small and practical because once you start, you are not likely to stop there. As you move ahead be careful not to become so mesmerized by the immediate stride taken that you forget the broad horizon. Sometimes we don't achieve all of our hopes, but dreamers who work at it don't fail, even though complete success may not be achieved.

Let me give you a practical example of something in its first steps—a program in which you might be able to assist.

I spoke at the University of Oregon and President David Frohnmayer and his wife Lynn had about ten people to their home for lunch. Someone asked me what the university might be able to contribute to the larger world picture in a concrete way.

I responded that I had just been thinking of a special need and I gave him an assignment. (Now that I am teaching, I am good at that.)

First, I offered a little background. In 1976 our nation celebrated its bicentennial and we had flags and bunting and grandiose speeches, but nothing to lift the vision of the nation. In the year 2009 we will celebrate the 200th birthday of Abraham Lincoln. While he is rightfully remembered primarily for freeing the slaves, he also signed into law the Morrill Act, giving federal assistance to the land grant colleges. His predecessor, James Buchanan, had vetoed the bill. That action by President Lincoln caused the greatest stride forward in higher education in the nineteenth century, just as the GI Bill of 1944 did in the twentieth century.

If we could lift our vision and do something significant in higher education as a tribute to Lincoln, we would have both the enrichment of reflecting on our history and a thrust forward for the nation.

September 11th did not happen in a vacuum. Our insensitivity to the rest of the world, growing out of ignorance, comes across to other nations as arrogance. The fate of Americans is inextricably tied to the fate of people in other countries.

As of this writing, we have 584,000 international students in our colleges and universities—good for them and good for us. However, only slightly more than one percent of our students study abroad for a summer or a semester, and two-thirds of them study in Western Europe, while 95 percent of the world's population growth in the next fifty years will be in the developing nations.

What if we had a grant program for students going into their junior year of college who have maintained at least a "B" average, permitting them to study abroad for a summer or a semester, with preference given to those hoping to do this academic work in the developing nations. I suggest the junior year in college so the students can return for at least one year to their campuses and bring more of an international flavor to their schools. If we were to make up to a $7,000 grant available to five hundred thousand students every year, the cost would be $3.5 billion—less than the cost of three B-2 bombers, and it would do infinitely more for the future security of our nation than those bombers. That $3.5 billion would be one-seventh of one percent of the federal budget, or one thirty-fourth of the increase in the defense expenditure in fiscal year 2003. It is $400 million less than we are spending in Iraq each month. In ten years we would have five million Americans who had studied abroad. That would inevitably lead to more sensitive and sophisticated leadership in the U.S.

David Hubin in the University of Oregon's president's office is heading the effort there. Lynn Frohnmayer, the president's wife, has worked abroad and immediately struck me as a dynamic person who could assist in this; she is part of the committee. I talked to a former president of Columbia University, Michael Sovern, and he is enthusiastic about the idea. So are Father Theodore Hesburgh, former president of Notre Dame; John Brademas, former president of New York University; George Rupp, former president of Columbia University and president of Brandeis University. Just today I received a phone call today from Duke University showing interest. I hope that by the time this book comes out, Congress will have inched forward on this. Somehow we have to keep this dream alive.

Will we be successful? If I didn't think we had a chance I wouldn't be suggesting it. At the very worst, we will have caused serious discussion about our international studies deficiencies and in some small way we will move forward a little.

But we have a chance to do something exciting. At the University of Oregon they are putting meat on the skeleton of an idea. They are dreaming.

And we will become a better nation because of their dreams.

If you like the concept, you can help to make this dream become a reality by writing to your House and Senate members in Washington, or helping in some other concrete way that fits your circumstances.

WE CRAVE LEADERSHIP that appeals to our ideals—even as we tell pollsters that we want a tax cut and other things that cater to our greed rather than helping future generations or the rest of the world. And yet—not surprisingly—pollsters who phrase their questions differently come up with dramatically different answers. Do people want a big tax cut? Yes. Do people favor a smaller tax cut and more money going into education? Yes. Health care delivery? Yes. Health care research? Yes. The list goes on. However, polls won't produce a dream.

We want leadership that talks straight and looks to the future. That could emerge from the top, as in the case of President Harry Truman. But it is more likely to happen if people at the grass roots level tell political leaders that we expect more than pandering, that we yearn for leadership that urges the nation to strive for lofty goals. We need to tell those who lead that we are willing to sacrifice for such purposes. Remember the words on baseball great Jackie Robinson's tomb: "The value of life is measured by its impact on other lives." To have that impact will require more than conversation. Comedian George Burns said: "Too bad that all the people who know how to run the country are busy driving taxicabs and cutting hair."[5] Talking about issues and the course of the nation is better than not talking. But talking is not a substitute for action.

It will not take hundreds of thousands of people to cause positive movement. A handful in each congressional district and in each state can reenergize us. I hope you will be among that handful who help to change the course of history for the better.

You can help the nation heal itself.

You can help the nation dream once again.

NOTES

1. Equality

1. Quoted by John Woodworth, "How Should an Unrivaled Super-power Behave?" *Miller Center Report*, University of Virginia, Spring 2001.

2. Mark Shields, "American Politics Before and After 9-11," *Miller Center Report*, University of Virginia, Spring 2002.

3. Quoted in *Thomas Jefferson*, by Nathan Schachner (New York: Thomas Yoseloff, 1957), 252.

4. *Our Nation's Archive*, ed. Erik Bruun and Jay Crosby (New York: Black Dog and Leventhal, 1999), 199.

5. Alexis de Tocqueville, *Democracy in America*, originally published in 1835 (New York: Knopf, 1945), 1:35.

6. Ibid., 1:261.

7. Ibid., 1:256.

8. David Walker, "Appeals to the Colored Citizens of the World," in *Our Nation's Archive*, 231.

9. Carol Moseley-Braun, "Haven for Humanity," in *I Like Being American*, ed. Michael Leach (New York: Doubleday, 2003), 31.

10. Alice Duer Miller, reprinted in *Feminist Classics*, ed. Meg Bowman, (San Jose, Calif.: Hot Flash Press, 1994).

11. Quoted in "Republicans Like Gore's Choice but Liken Him More to Them than to Gore," by Adam Clymer, *New York Times*, 8 August 2000.

12. Quoted in "World Scan," *The Lutheran*, August 2002.

13. Quoted in *The Americans*, by J. C. Furnas (New York: Putnam, 1969), 524.

14. *Collected Works of Abraham Lincoln*, ed. Roy Basler (New Brunswick, N.J.: Rutgers University Press, 1953), 2:323.

15. Robert McChesney, "Immigration and Terrorism," *America*, 29 October 2001.

16. Daniel T. Griwold, "NAFTA Has Soundly Refuted Its Critics," *Chicago Sun-Times*, 27 December 2002.

17. Statement made during presidential debates of 1992.

18. George Gilder, "Geniuses from Abroad," *Wall Street Journal*, 18 December 1995.

19. Raymond Bonner, "New Policy Delays Visas for Specified Muslim Men," *New York Times*, 10 September 2002.

20. Tocqueville, *Democracy in America*, 1:270.

21. David McCullough, *Truman* (New York: Simon and Schuster, 1992), 651.

22. Letter to Emily Taft Douglas, 27 June 1957, quoted in *Crusading Liberal: Paul H. Douglas of Illinois*, by Roger Biles (Northern Illinois University Press: De Kalb, 2002), 120.

23. Edwardsville, Illinois, 11 September 1858, *Collected Works of Abraham Lincoln*, 3:95.

2. Religion

1. From *Lacon*, in *A New Dictionary of Quotations*, ed. H. L. Mencken (New York: Knopf, 1966), 1018.

2. Tocqueville, *Democracy in America*, 1:37.

3. Ibid., 1:39.

4. Ibid., 1:303, 307.

5. Ibid., 1:308.

6. Forrest Church, interview with Bill Moyers, *A World of Ideas* (New York: Doubleday, 1989), 411.

7. Quoted in *Lutheranism in America*, by Abdel Wentz (Philadelphia: Muhlenberg Press, 1955), 116.

8. Quotations from Pat Robertson ("Nazis"), Franklin Graham ("wicked religion"), and Jerry Vines ("pedophile"), past president of the Southern Baptist Convention.

9. Paul Weyrich and William Lind, *Why Islam Is a Threat to America and the West* (Washington: Free Congress Foundation, 2002), 1.

10. Associated Press, "GOP Official Apologizes for Sending Article," *St. Louis Post-Dispatch*, 6 January 2003. The article that was the subject

of this newspaper story was written by William Lind, who co-authored the pamphlet on Islam. The official who apologized for sending Lind's article, William Back, is vice chair of the California Republican party.

11. Thomas Paine, "Common Sense," in *Our Nation's Archive*, 126.

12. Samuel F. B. Morse, "The Dangers from Popery," in *Our Nation's Archive*, 244.

13. Nicholas Kristof, "Stoning in Scripture," *New York Times*, 30 April 2002.

14. Barbara Crosette, "Study Warns of Stagnation in Arab Societies," *New York Times*, 2 July 2002.

15. "War in Afghanistan," unsigned editorial, *America*, 29 October 2001.

16. Carlotta Gall, "Half a Million Are Left Homeless in Afghan Cities as Winter Bites," *New York Times*, 2 January 2003.

17. "Politics Is a Contact Sport," lecture by Alan Simpson, University of California, Irvine, May 2002.

18. David McCullough, *John Adams* (New York: Simon and Schuster, 2001), 354.

19. Elaine Pagels, interview with Bill Moyers, *A World of Ideas*, 386.

20. Quoted in obituary, "Bob Jones Jr., 86, University Chancellor," *Chicago Tribune*, 13 November 1997.

21. Quoted in *Teaching Tolerance*, by Sara Bullard (New York: Doubleday, 1996), 85.

22. Eugene McCarthy and Keith Burris, "The Singular Piety of Politics," *New York Times*, 31 August 2000.

23. Robert Whitcomb, "Life Isn't All About Investments," *Providence Journal*, reprinted in the *St. Louis Post-Dispatch*, 11 July 2002.

24. Quoted in *Partnership or Peril*, by Oliver Thomas (Nashville: First Amendment Center, 2001), 4.

25. Ulysses S. Grant, Seventh Annual Message to Congress, 7 December 1875.

26. Ulysses S. Grant, Message to the Society of the Army of the Tennessee, Des Moines, Iowa, September 30, 1875.

27. Napoleon, letter to Count Antoine Thibaudeau, June 1801, in *Dictionary of Quotations*, ed. H. L. Mencken (New York: Knopf, 1942), 1018.

28. Robert Putnam, *Bowling Alone* (New York: Simon and Schuster, 2000), 67.

29. Article VII, Section 4.

30. Constitution of the State of Massachusetts, 1780, in *Dictionary of Quotations*, 1205.

31. John Ferguson, "Religion in Public Schools? Who Decides?" *Liberty*, May/June 2001.

32. Rob Boston, "The Good Old Days," *Liberty*, January/February 1999.

33. Barna Research, quoted in "News and Views," by Daniel Roth, Southern Illinois District supplement, *Lutheran Witness*, August 2002.

34. Statistics cited in "Politics Without Piety," by Geoffrey Wheatcroft, *New York Times*, 9 September 2000.

35. Sue Simpson, quoted in *Moral Freedom*, by Alan Wolfe (New York: Norton, 2001), 14.

36. Hannah Arendt, *Between Past and Future* (New York: Viking, 1961), 95.

37. Putnam, *Bowling Alone*, 72.

38. *A Call to Civil Society: Why Democracy Needs Moral Truths* (New York: Institute for American Values, 1998), 15.

39. Forrester Church, *The Seven Deadly Virtues* (New York: Harper and Row, 1988), 27.

40. Martin Luther King Jr., *A Call to Conscience*, ed. Clayborne Carson and Kris Shepard (New York: Warner Books, 2001), 96.

41. "The Fight for God," *The Economist*, 21 December 2002.

42. From Dag Hammerskjöld's book, *Markings*, quoted in *The Third Freedom*, by George McGovern (New York: Simon and Schuster, 2001), 45.

3. The World Family

1. Quoted in *It Takes A Village*, by Hillary Clinton (New York: Simon and Schuster, 1996), 109.

2. Ephesians 3:14.

3. Quoted in *A New Dictionary of Quotations*, 385.

4. Quoted in *The Third Best Things Ever Said*, by Robert Byrne (New York, Atheneum, 1986), 248.

5. Press release, Institute for American Values, New York City, 14 February 2002.

6. William Burrows, "American Values Abroad," *Sightings*, 10 October 2001.

7. Quoted in *Columbia Dictionary of Quotations*, ed. Robert Andrews, (New York: Columbia University Press, 1993), 315.

8. Al and Tipper Gore, *Joined at the Heart* (New York: Henry Holt, 2002), 324.

9. Ellen Goodman, "We Value At-home Moms, Unless They're Single and Poor," *St. Louis Post-Dispatch*, May 26, 2002.

10. Putnam, *Bowling Alone*, 272–273.

11. Ibid., 98–101.

12. DDB Needham Life Style Survey, quoted in *Bowling Alone*, by Robert Putnam, 100.

13. Putnam, *Bowling Alone*, 212.

14. Ibid., 101.

4. Restraint

1. Wolfe, *Moral Freedom*, 74.

2. Moyers, *A World of Ideas*, 412.

3. Nathaniel Whittaker, quoted in *The Seven Deadly Virtues*, by Forrester Church, 48.

4. Daniel Boorstin, *Hidden History* (New York: Harper and Row, 1987), 94.

5. Schachner, *Thomas Jefferson*, 380.

6. William Julius Wilson, interview with Bill Moyers, *A World of Ideas*, 78.

7. Quoted in *An Ethic for Enemies*, by Donald W. Shriver Jr. (New York: Oxford University Press, 1995), 8.

8. David Wise, "Why the Spooks Shouldn't Run Wars," *Time*, 3 February 2003.

9. Quoted in "Truman Got It Right," by Mike Moore, *Bulletin of the Atomic Scientists*, January/February 2003.

10. Ibid.

11. Quoted in "Publisher's Note," by Wendy McFadden, *The Messenger* (Church of the Brethren publication), November 2001.

12. King, *A Call to Conscience*, 157.

5. Participation

1. Quoted in *It Takes a Village*, by Hillary Clinton, 20.

2. Tocqueville, *Democracy in America*, 1:243–244.

3. Ibid., 2:107.

4. Statistics vary slightly. These are used by Harold W. Stanle and Richard Niemi in *Vital Statistics on American Politics*, 2001–2002 (Washington: C. Q. Press, 2001), 12–13.

5. 1998 statistics compiled by the Institute for Democracy and Electoral Assistance, Sweden.

6. Roper poll, quoted in *Bowling Alone*, by Robert Putnam, 36.

7. Putnam, *Bowling Alone*, 36.

8. Midge Miller, "Citizens, Like Parents, Must Provide a Guiding Hand," *Capital Times*, Madison, Wis., 7–8 July 2001.

9. Quoted in undated paper by David Christensen, Southern Illinois University.

10. Putnam, *Bowling Alone*, 42.

11. Ibid., 46.

12. Susan Crawford and Peggy Levitt, "Social Change and Civic Engagement: The Case of the PTA," quoted in *Bowling Alone*, by Robert Putnam, 56.

13. Putnam, *Bowling Alone*, 72.

14. Ibid., 75.

15. Ibid., 118.

16. Al Franken, *Oh, the Things I Know* (New York: Dutton, 2002), xiv.

17. Tocqueville, *Democracy in America*, 1:243.

6. Education

1. From *The Outline of History*, in *Columbia Dictionary of Quotations*, 267.

2. John Adams, "Thoughts on Government," quoted in *John Adams*, by David McCullough, 103.

3. Tocqueville, *Democracy in America*, 1:203, 309.

4. Ibid., 1:200.

5. Rosalind Rossi, "Poor Students Shortchanged," *Chicago Sun-Times*, 8 January 2003.

6. Tocqueville, *Democracy in America*, 2:35.

7. Tracey King and Ellynne Bannon, *The Burden of Borrowing* (Washington, D.C.: State PIRG [Public Interest Research Group] Higher Education Project, 2002), 1.

8. *Losing Ground* (Washington, D.C.: National Center for Public Policy and Higher Education, 2002), 9.

9. Ibid., 5.

10. Related by Vartan Gregorian, interview with Bill Moyers, *A World of Ideas*, 188.

11. Gregorian, interview with Bill Moyers, *A World of Ideas*, 188.

12. David Gergen, *Eyewitness to Power* (New York: Simon and Schuster, 2000), 42–43.

13. Gregorian, 183.

14. Quoted in *The Imperial Mantle*, by David Newsom (Bloomington: Indiana University Press, 2001), 7.

15. *What We're Fighting For* (New York: Institute for American Values, 2002), 1.

7. Optimism

1. From *What is America?* by Arthur Goodfriend, in *Book of Twentieth Century American Quotations*, ed. Stephen Donadio et al. (New York: Warner Books, 1992), 266.

2. "Booting Out the Big Men," unsigned editorial, *The Economist*, 21 December 2002.

3. *Sangamo Journal*, 15 March 1832.

4. Quoted in *Columbia Dictionary of Quotations*, 655.

8. Respect for the Law

1. Quoted in "Nevada Blazes Trail for Legal Marijuana," by V. Dion Haynes, *Chicago Tribune*, 9 August 2002.

2. Robert McChesney, "Immigration and Terrorism," *America*, 29 October 2001.

3. "Michigan Officials Want to Talk with 550 Men in State from Mideast," *St. Louis Post-Dispatch*, 27 November 2001.

4. Forrest Church, quoted in *A World of Ideas*, by Bill Moyers, 420.

5. Quoted in "Inside the First Amendment: Graduation 2002: One Stark Lesson in Freedom," by Ken Paulson, Gannett News Service, 3 June 2002.

6. King, *A Call to Conscience*, 32.

7. Tocqueville, *Democracy in America*, 1:245.

8. American Bar Association statistics, quoted in "The Blotter," *Black Issues in Higher Education*, 17 January 2002.

9. Quoted in *St. Louis Post-Dispatch* editorial, "America Behind Bars," 18 August 2001.

10. Clarence Page, "When Prisons Lure More than Colleges," *Chicago Tribune*, 1 September 2002.

11. "The Prevalence of Co-Occurring Mental Illness and Substance Use Disorders in Jails," *Bulletin of the Substance Abuse and Mental Health Services Administration*, Spring 2002.

12. Mary Dudziak, "Giving Capital Offense," *Civilization*, October/November 2000.

13. Studies are quoted in "The Deterrent Effect of the Death Penalty: Facts v. Faiths," by Hans Zeisel, *Supreme Court Review*, 1976.

14. Quoted in "The Deterrent Effect of the Death Penalty," by Hans Zeisel.

15. Quoted in "Citing Money Concerns, Judge Rejects Death Penalty," by Adam Piptak, *New York Times*, 18 August 2002.

16. Jesse L. Jackson Sr., Jesse L. Jackson Jr., and Bruce Shapiro, in "Executioners' Song," *New York Times* Book Review, 7 October 2001, quoted from their book, *Legal Lynching*.

17. Hans Zeisel, "Race Bias in the Administration of the Death Penalty: The Florida Experience," *Harvard Law Review*, Vol. 95 (1981): 456.

18. Report to the American Bar Association by David Baldus, 1998.

19. "Juveniles and the Death Penalty: Executions Worldwide Since 1990," Amnesty International, 11 January 1998. Retrieved from the World Wide Web 28 August 2002. <http://www.web.amnesty.org/ai.nsf/index/ACT500111998>

20. Quoted in *Democracy in America*, by Alexis de Tocqueville, 2:165.

21. Tocqueville, *Democracy in America*, 2:166.

22. Ibid., 1:272.

23. Quoted in *Columbia Dictionary of Quotations*, 508.

24. *Missouri Republican*, May 26, 1836.

25. Ibid.

26. *Collected Works of Abraham Lincoln*, 1:112.

9. Humility

1. Cicero, *De officis*, I, 78 B.C.E.

2. Weyrich and Lind, *Why Islam Is a Threat to America and the West*, 1.

3. Quoted in *Lincoln's Virtues*, by William Lee Miller (New York: Knopf, 2002), 85.

4. Benjamin Franklin, 1735, in *Dictionary of Quotations*, 557.

5. Quoted in *The Seven Deadly Virtues*, by Forrester Church, 46.

6. Tocqueville, *Democracy in America*, 1:242.

7. John Woodworth, "How Should an Unrivalled Superpower Behave?," *Miller Center Report*, University of Virginia, Spring 2002.

8. Newsom, *The Imperial Mantle*, 201.

10. Compassion

1. Catherine Bowen, *Miracle at Philadelphia* (Boston: Little, Brown, 1966), 73–74.

2. Quoted in *John Adams*, by David McCullough, 21.

3. Letter, Hope Marston to Paul Simon, 30 April 2002.

4. Tocqueville, *Democracy in America*, 1:208.

5. State of the Union message, 1988.

6. McGovern, *The Third Freedom*, 69–70.

7. Quoted in "Editor's Note," by Peter Passell, *Miliken Institute Review*, Third Quarter 2001.

8. Quoted in *Wealth and Democracy*, by Kevin Phillips (New York: Broadway Books, 2002), 47.

9. Quoted in *Wealth and Democracy*, by Kevin Phillips, 396.

10. Robert Pear, "Number of People Living in Poverty Increases in U.S.," *New York Times*, 25 September 2002.

11. David Horovitz, "While Jerusalem Burns," *Jerusalem Report*, 30 December 2002.

12. J. Bryan Hehir, "Realistic Hope As We Struggle," *National Catholic Reporter*, 16 August 2002.

13. Quoted in *Best Practices*, ed. Shelby Coffey III (Washington: Freedom Forum, 2002), 35.

14. Quoted in *A Nation Lost and Found*, ed. Frank Pierson and Stanley K. Scheinbaum (Los Angeles: Tallfellow Press), 34.

15. Karen DeYoung, "Giving Less: The Decline in Foreign Aid," *Washington Post*, 25 November 1999.

16. Somini Sengupta, "U.N. Prepares For a Debate on Dire Needs of Children," *New York Times*, 8 May 2002.

17. Moyers, *A World of Ideas*, 221.

18. Henry Steele Commager, interview with Bill Moyers, *A World of Ideas*, 223.

19. Peter Peterson, "Public Diplomacy and the War on Terrorism," a condensation of the Task Force report, *Foreign Affairs*, September/October 2002.

20. George Will, "Politics Trumps Pakistan's Loyalty," *Chicago Sun-Times*, 14 April 2002.

21. Newsom, *The Imperial Mantle*, 201–202.

22. Speech given in October 2002, quoted in *Bread for the World Newsletter*, December 2002.

23. Bob Kerrey, "The Challenge of Freedom," *Parade Magazine*, 12 May 2002.

24. Quoted in *Truman*, by David McCullough, 583.

25. Quoted in *A World of Ideas*, by Bill Moyers, 417.

26. Quoted by President George H. W. Bush, State of the Union message, 9 February 1989.

11. Courage

1. Michel Eyquem de Montaigne, "Essay III," in *The Essays in Great Books of the Western World*, ed. Robert Hutchins (Chicago: Encyclopedia Brittanica, 1952), in *A New Dictionary of Quotations*, 227.

2. Speech in New York City, 29 May 1882, *A New Dictionary of Quotations*, 228.

3. Quoted in *America: A Library of Original Sources* (Chicago: Veterans of Foreign Wars, 1925), 3:188.

4. Paul Kennedy, *Preparing for the Twenty-First Century* (New York: Random House, 1993), 324.

5. David McCullough, "The Argonauts of 1776," *New York Times*, 4 July 2002.

6. Quoted by Henry Steele Commager, interview with Bill Moyers, *A World of Ideas*, 222.

7. C. S. Lewis, quoted in *Columbia Dictionary of Quotations*, 191.

8. Andrew Young, quoted in *A Call to Conscience*, 4.

9. McCullough, *Truman*, 360.

12. Protection of Our Earth

1. From *Letters From an American Farmer*, in *A New Dictionary of Quotations*, 352.

2. Luther Standing Bear, *Land of the Spotted Eagle* (Boston: Houghton Mifflin, 1933), 165–166.

3. Tocqueville, *Democracy in America*, 2:236.

4. 1493 letter quoted in *The Environmental Debate, A Documentary History*, ed. Penninah Neimark and Peter Rhoades Mott (Westport, Conn: Greenwood Press, 1999), 27–28.

5. *The Environmental Debate*, 189.

6. Daniel Eisenberg, "Is This Any Way to Run a Railroad?" *Time*, 3 December 2001.

7. Kennedy, *Preparing for the Twenty-First Century*, 190, quoting from the *Boston Globe*, 20 December 1989, and *The Economist*, 6 October 1990.

13. Integrity

1. From *The History of Rasselas*, in *Columbia Dictionary of Quotations*, 465.

2. Quoted in *Eyewitness to Power*, by David Gergen, 139.

3. Hannah Arendt, quoted in *Moral Freedom*, by Alan Wolfe, 111.

4. Barbara Tuchman, interview with with Bill Moyers, *A World of Ideas*, 6.

14. And...

1. John M. Buchanan, "Who Cares?" *Christian Century*, 11 January 2003.

2. "An Uncertain Trumpet," *New York Times*, 8 September 2002.

3. Mark Shields, "American Politics Before and After 9-11," *Miller Center Report*, University of Virginia, Spring 2002.

4. Tuchman, interview with with Bill Moyers, *A World of Ideas*, 7.

5. *Life* magazine, December 1979, in *Book of Twentieth Century Quotations*, 185.

INDEX